TIME TRAVEL – FACT NOT FICTION

Time Slips, Real Time Machines

And How-To Experiments To Go

Forwards and Backwards Through Time

Commander X

&

Tim R. Swartz

Global Communications

TIME TRAVEL – FACT NOT FICTION

Time Slips, Real Time Machines And How-To Experiments
To Go Forwards and Backwards Through Time

By Commander X and Tim R. Swartz

Nonfiction

ISBN-13: 978-1606111352
ISBN-10: 1606111353

Manufactured in the United States of America

Timothy G. Beckley, Editorial Director
Assistant to Publisher, Carol Ann Rodriguez
Editorial Assistants: Sean Casteel, William Kern

Free Catalog From:

Global Communications

Box 753,

New Brunswick, NJ 08903

mrufo8@hotmail.com

Visit our website at:

www.conspiracyjournal.com

Contents

Introduction

It has been the dream of philosopher and scientist alike. The fantasies of every small boy and the musings of writers and poets throughout the ages; to be able to shed the shackles of seconds, minutes and hours, to go beyond the confines of today and the shadows of yesterday.

Time travel...the very words seem to conjure up the infinite possibilities of the past and future revealed. This might seem like a subject of science fiction, but it encourages much thought in matters both physical and philosophical. A recent paper in Scientific American discussed whether time travel is indeed feasible and why current physical and philosophical objections don't preclude the possibility of time travel.

Most scientists, who have not seriously studied the works of Einstein, Hawking's and others, dismiss time travel as unscientific, with as much validity as the lurid accounts of abductions by extraterrestrials.

On the other hand, proponents of time travel point out that Einstein's equations for general relativity do allow some forms of time travel. In fact, we are all travelers in time, at a rate, by earthly standards, of 24 hours a day, continuously. This progress, at a constant speed and in a fixed direction (toward the future), is never-ending and unchangeable.

Time travel is any deviation from this steady, unchanging progress. Can we move forward at a faster rate? Arriving in the future long before our friends who remain plodding along at 24 hours per day? Can we slow our own passage through time and be left behind by our more "constant" friends? Or the most exciting possibility of all, can we travel at will forwards or backwards through time like the hero of H.G. Wells' definitive book, The Time Machine?

Whether by mechanical means like the controversial Montauk Project, or by using the untapped powers of the human mind, time travel is a reality that offers mankind the potential of freedom from the limitations of our linear universe. A universe that can now be opened to the fullest, revealing the beauties and mysteries of our existence.

Time Travel – Fact Not Fiction

Time travel is a reality that offers mankind the potential of freedom from the limitations of our linear universe. A universe that can now be opened to the fullest, revealing the beauties and mysteries of our existence.

Chapter One
The Mysteries Of Time

Professor Stephen Hawking, Britain's leading cosmic physicist, has accepted the possibility of time travel. Having ridiculed the concept for years, Hawking now says that it is not just a possibility but one on which the government should spend money.

Not that long ago, Hawking, the world-famous professor of mathematics at Cambridge University, stirred up debate between cosmologists and astronomers when he dismissed time travel. This came as a growing number of astronomers and physicists were speculating that Einstein's general theory of relativity might allow for the possibility.

Hawking, however, produced his chronology protection hypothesis, a mixture of advanced science and ordinary logic. Time travel, he said, would allow people to alter their own pasts. You could murder your ancestors or even prevent your own birth, a possibility he considered ridiculous.

"The best evidence that time travel will never be possible is that we have not been invaded by hordes of tourists from the future," he said several years ago.

Now, in the forward to the book, *The Physics of Star Trek*, by American astronomer Lawrence Krauss, Hawking has recanted to the point of adopting the language of the popular TV show. He talks openly of warping space and of faster-than-light travel.

He said: "One of the consequences of rapid interstellar travel would be that one could also go back in time."

Hawking said he still thinks time travel would probably never be practical, but the seeds of doubt had been sown in his mind: "If you combine Einstein's general theory of relativity with quantum theory, it does begin to seem a possibility."

He pointed out that research on "closed time-like curves," the technical term for time travel, is going on in a number of universities, including Cambridge and the California Institute of Technology. "It

Time Travel – Fact Not Fiction

doesn't involve much money - what it needs is an openness of mind to consider possibilities that might appear fantastic."

Scientific debate over time travel goes back to Sir Isaac Newton who, in the 17th century, dismissed it completely; claiming that time and space were fixed and immutable. His assertions were accepted until Einstein showed that time and space is closely related and that both are affected by gravity. His theories led to the idea that enormous gravitational fields, such as those found around collapsing stars, known as black holes, could reverse the flow of time.

Dr. Michio Kaku, a professor of theoretical physics at the City University of New York, who is touring Britain to publicize his new book, also supports time travel - in theory.

"Building a genuine time machine will not be as easy as sitting in a chair and twirling a few knobs. Modern proposals for such a machine face one severe problem: the energy supply," he said.

He believes that the necessary energy will only be found in fuel sources located in outer space, which still leaves the problem of getting there.

As Hawking says in his foreword: "There is a two-way trade between science fiction and science. We may not yet be able to boldly go where no man or woman has gone before, but at least we can do it in the mind."

What Is Time?

Time and space have fascinated man since the dawn of civilization. People have spent eons thinking about these concepts and the ideas behind them. The Greeks, the Romans, the English, all have stared at the heavens and wondered about the mysteries of time.

Think what it would be like to be able to freely travel down the back roads of time; maybe to visit a famous event such as a historic battle. Imagine gazing down over the fields of Kent and seeing the arrow that struck King Harold in 1066, or to see the Great Exhibition of 1851. Imagine walking down the central aisle of this amazing glasshouse and seeing firsthand the latest works of art and science from around the world, or to solve a historical mystery. Imagine watching the visit of President Kennedy to Dallas in November 1963 to see if anybody really was on the grassy knoll, or to travel back to a time where the countryside is untouched by the hand of man. To walk on a sunny summer day through a meadow full of wild flowers down to a bubbling clear water stream, or to travel to the future to witness events yet to happen, to see new discoveries and inventions, to see the future of mankind. As the boundaries of science are pushed further back, it is becoming clear that whoever understands the laws of physics best will be able to travel through time and space, easily gaining a dominant position in the known universe. Indeed the race which can move from universe to universe will get to control all know universes situated in Time and Space. One commonly accepted definition of time comes from the ancient world. It says that time is "the measure of motion." This is inadequate for two reasons. First, time is itself insufficient to measure motion, since motion is measured in terms of both Time and Space. That is, a physical event has both temporal and spatial extensions.

Second, it is conceivable that time could be used to measure nonphysical events, absent of motion. Time is necessary for change, but locative change is restricted to the physical world, whereas some changes occur apart from that or are at least distinct from it. The proposed definition was probably attractive due to the correlation between every motion and the existence of time. It fails to consider the dual nature of motion and the broader applications of time. Aristotle made almost the same point when he argued that tying the idea of time to motion alone was problematic and that it should also be considered a measure of rest.

If we believe that time moves, then we might have to answer questions such as "what moves it?" and "how does it know how fast to go?" One strange result that is widely noted but rarely explored is that if time moves and bears some relation to reality, then in some manner, it would be the cause of our motion, for don't we say that a deceleration of time would result in our own deceleration, and that if it were to accelerate, we would speed up? And if it were to stop, we stop?

Such transformations are considered all embracing, such that no system of molecular motions, or indeed anyone's consciousness, is left undisturbed, in which case, a variance in the rate of time would have no impact on the relative state of one thing to another. Thus, there would be no way to scientifically monitor such changes. But if time moves, what is stopping it from altering its rate of motion?

Popular notions view time as like an ever-flowing river, with the present as a raft floating on this river, and we, as a conscious observer, are riding upon this raft. The past would be what was behind the raft and the future is what is in front of the raft. This view of time, however, is simplistic and probably erroneous. Eastern philosophies have told us that time is an illusion, that the past, present and future exist simultaneously; sort of a constant state of NOW. This is difficult to contemplate for those who have been reared in the western world. Western materialism teaches that the universe is basically mechanical in nature. That reality works rather like the gears in a clock or machine.

Of course, we now know that time as we perceive it is a construct of the mind, brought about by the physical realities of the world around us. The sun rises and sets. The moon travels across the sky, changing its appearance throughout the month. Because of these factors, our condition has dictated that physical reality be broken down into units of measurements - seconds, minutes, hours, days, weeks, months, years etc. However, these units of measurements are purely arbitrary. They have no real meaning.

Space is three-dimensional, but spatially so. This is a strange but significant qualification because we also speak of time as a dimension, only a temporal one, and the distinction (and similarity) is important to recognize.

Though these two ideas are dryly commonplace, we can, even with this as a starting point, begin to notice some interesting points. We said that time is a dimension, but not merely dimensional. Presumably, the predication of the term for time comes from our immediate assumption that it is one-dimensional.

While we speak of space as possessing the property of three dimensionality, we rarely discuss that fact. It may be that, when speaking of space, most people are interested in communicating the specific number of its directional extensions and are less concerned with the label itself. For the purposes of this discussion, it is important to keep in mind that it is a type of dimension, and that, in addition to this predication, it is three-dimensional. Thus, so far, we have declared the spatial and temporal dimensions.

Space itself seems devoid of substance. It does not occupy anything but is that in which things are occupied. What kind of entity can be but be without substance? Perhaps the spatial dimension is no more than dimension itself. This is something that has confounded scientist and philosopher alike.

Since time does not seem to have a tangible substance, then it may also qualify for this description. It may be that the best way to understand the meaning of dimension is to view it as a precondition for other things, itself nothing more than an empty container. If space is really "nothing," then it cannot undergo modifications. When a thing moves through space, space does not also move. As the temporal dimension, time would really be "nothing" in itself but merely a precondition for other things. The ordinary perception of the passage of time is an illusion we are accustomed to, inadvertently associating time with the motions of orbiting planets and timepiece hands, a useful practice to measure temporal displacements – motion (of things) in time.

We often think of space as static and time as dynamic. However, in the dimension-theory, both are static, for it is objects that move, passing through those dimensions in which they exist. One may argue that while an object may be able to remain still in space (macroscopically speaking), things cannot remain still in time. But wouldn't a thing be stationary in time if it met the condition that it did not change?

If there is no change, then time becomes "nothing to it." It is as with space where one exists without a body: space would be "nothing to it." One would not be "in space." If we did not change, we would not experience space and time as we do. Space does not constrain bodiless things, and time would have no purpose for an immutable being.

This is exactly what we have been hearing over the centuries from those who have claimed contact with the spiritual worlds. Those who dwell in the realm of spirit say that time is meaningless to them. Only in the constantly changing world of physical reality does time and space have any meaning.

According to the late Jane Roberts, who allegedly channeled a spiritual being by the name of Seth, time as we experience it is an illusion caused by our own physical senses. These senses force us to perceive action in certain terms, but this is not the nature of action. The apparent boundaries between past, present and future are only illusions caused by the amount of action we can physically perceive, and so it seems to us that one moment exists and is gone forever, and the next moment comes and like the one before, also disappears. Everything in the universe exists at one time simultaneously.

The first words ever spoken still ring through the universe, and in our terms, the last words ever spoken have already been said. The past, present and future only appear to those who exist within three-dimensional reality. The past exists as a series of electromagnetic connections held in the physical brain and in the nonphysical mind. These electromagnetic connections can be changed. The future consists of a series of electromagnetic connections in the mind and brain also. In other words, the past and present are real to the same extent. We take it for granted that present action can change the future, but present actions can also change the past.

The past is no more objective or independent from the perceiver than is the present. The electromagnetic connections were largely made by the individual perceiver. The connection can be changed, and such changes are far from uncommon. These changes happen spontaneously on a subconscious basis. The past is seldom what we remember it to be, for we have already rearranged it from the instant of any given event. The past is being constantly re-created by each individual as attitudes and associations change. This is an actual recreation, not a symbolic one. The child is indeed still within the man, but he is not the child that "was," for even the child within the man constantly changes. Difficulties arise when such alterations do not occur automatically. Severe neurosis is often caused precisely because an individual has not changed his past.

A change of attitude, a new association, or any of the innumerable other actions will automatically set up new electromagnetic connections and break others. Every action changes every other action. Therefore, every action in our present affects actions we call past.

It is possible to react in the past to an event that has not occurred, and to be influenced by our own future. It is also possible for an individual to react in the past to an event in the future, which in your terms, may never occur.

Because past, present and future exist simultaneously, there is no reason why we cannot react to an event whether or not it happens to fall within the small field of reality in which we usually observe and participate. On a subconscious level, we react to many events that have not yet occurred as far as our ego's awareness is concerned.

Such reactions are carefully screened out and not admitted to consciousness. The ego finds such instances distracting and annoying, and when forced to admit their validity, will resort to the most far-fetched rationalizations to explain them. No event is predestined. Any given event can be changed not only before and during but after its occurrence.

The individual is hardly at the mercy of past events, for he changes them constantly. He is hardly at the mercy of future events, for he changes these not only before, but also after their happening. An individual's future actions are not dependent upon a concrete finished past, for such a past never existed. The past is as real as the future, no more or less.

Time Travel – Fact Not Fiction

There is a part of us that is not locked within physical reality, and that part knows that there is only an Eternal Now. The part of us that knows is the whole self, our inner and outer ego (all that we are).

From within this framework we will see that physical time is as dreamlike as we once thought inner time was. We will discover our whole self, peeping inward and outward at the same "time," and find that all time is one time, and all divisions, illusions.

Our idea of space and time is determined by our neurological structure. The camouflage is so craftily executed and created by the inner self that we must, by necessity, focus our attention on the physical reality which has been created.

The single line of physical experience is merely the surface thread along which we seem to travel. In actuality, following this analogy, there would be an infinite number of threads both above and below your own, all part of one inconceivably miraculous web-work.

What is Reality?

In order to understand time, we must first ask just what exactly reality is. Is it a solid something that can be touched and physically manipulated? On the other hand, is it something intangible, with no more substance or influence then the mist on a spring morning? Beyond the question of whether or not reality is composed of one or more basic substance lies the question, what kind of substance is it.

On this issue, metaphysics traditionally has been divided between materialists who believe that all reality is basically material or physical and idealists who believe that reality is spiritual or non material. Important materialists have been the pre-Socratic atomists, Thomas Hobbes, and Karl Marx. Among contemporary materialist theories, especially with respect to the nature of humanity, are analytical behaviorism and the neural identity theory of mind. Major idealists have included Parmenides, Plato, George Berkeley, Johann Gottlieb Fichte, and Hegel.

A third major metaphysical issue centers around the problem of permanence and change. Except for some philosophers, like Parmenides, who have denied the reality of change, and others, like Heraclitus, who have denied the possibility of permanence, most philosophers have attempted to explain change in terms of either mechanism or Teleology. Materialists have tended to take a mechanistic view, explaining change as the action and reaction of physical particles with one another. Both idealists and theologians have taken a teleologic approach, appealing to a spiritual (usually supernatural) principle as the ultimate source and cause of all change. Plato's ideal "Forms," Spinoza's pantheistic "God," Hegel's "Absolute," and the Judeo-Christian God are examples of such principles. Aristotle worked out a naturalistic teleology, holding that every individual thing in the universe moves toward a goal inherent in its nature.

The modern attack on metaphysics began with the skeptical Empiricism of David Hume, who argued that ideas like "substance," "reality," "mind," and "causality" was not demonstrable. Kant, as well, questioned the possibility of metaphysical knowledge in the traditional sense. In his view, the ultimate nature of reality (things as they really are) is unknowable, for the human mind is limited to knowledge of phenomena or appearances.

His several critiques of the speculative and practical functions of reason significantly altered the course of philosophy. After Kant, philosophers such as Fichte and Hegel became more interested in the creative activity of the ego or reason itself than in the natural world. It was not long, however, before these newer systems came under severe attack from both Marx and the positivists, an attack from which idealism and metaphysics in general have never fully recovered.

In recent years, many philosophers have come to believe that only the natural sciences can legitimately investigate the nature of reality. Therefore, for many contemporary philosophers the proper philosophical endeavor is the analysis of language. Among the major metaphysicians remaining are phenomenologists and existentialists, whose concern with the unique existing self and the world of which it is immediately conscious stand in sharp contrast to the traditional concern with the nature of total or ultimate reality as it exists within or beyond experience itself. Yet, these philosophic musings do little to explain the mysterious events that occur daily in our world. Events that lead us to believe that reality and time are ever changing.

Chapter Two
Spontaneous Cases of Time Travel

Our world is a strange and mysterious place. How can we explain the unusual incidents that occur on a daily basis that seem to flaunt the apparent plastic nature of our reality?

Mysterious disappearances, out of place objects, sightings of people, buildings, even entire towns that seem to be "unstuck in time." All of these things show that time is not entirely moving in a straight line to the future, but, like a flowing stream, is filled with eddies and whirlpools. These whirlpools in time could explain many of the mysteries and unusual phenomena that have confounded humanity over the centuries.

People Caught In The Eddies Of Time

It is a sad fact that people disappear every day. Some are escaping from the law. Others are leaving an abusive relationship to start a fresh life. Children run away from home and vanish into the seamy world of drugs and prostitution. Some people have the misfortune to be in the wrong place at the wrong time, meet foul play and are never seen again. Then there are the cases of mysterious disappearances that offer no easy explanation. Some people seem to just "drop off the face of the earth." Are all of these people victims of kidnappers and murderers? Or, could they be victims of a natural event that is little understood by modern science. What really happens to these unfortunate individuals?

While physicists and other scientists look to technology to solve the riddle of time, they have often overlooked the possibilities that there are natural conditions that from time to time, seem to break down the barriers of Time and Space.

Over the centuries, there have been a number of strange stories of mysterious disappearances and the occasional reappearance. People, animals, even cars and buildings have vanished, never to be seen again. It is almost as if holes occasionally appear in the fabric of Time and Space. Those unlucky enough to be close enough to fall through disappear from this Time/Space. Almost instantly, some may fall out again, but find that they have been transported hundreds of miles from their starting point. Others, not so fortunate, may instead be transported across the dimension of time, perhaps to reappear months or even years in the past or future.

John Keel has cataloged a number of strange disappearances and reappearances in his book *Our Haunted Planet*. On October 24, 1967, Bruce Burkan found himself sitting in a bus terminal in Newark, New Jersey. He was dressed in a cheap suit with exactly seven cents in his pocket. He didn't have any idea what he was doing there, nor could he remember anything that had happened during the previous two months.

On August 22, 1967, Burkan and his girlfriend went to a beach at Asbury Park, New Jersey. He left her to go and put a coin in the parking meter. He was wearing nothing but a bathing suit. When he failed to return, his friend went looking for him. She found his locked car where he had parked it, but there was no sign of Burkan.

Burkan's family held a well-publicized search for him, but not a single clue turned up. Finally they conducted a funeral service in his memory, giving him up for dead. After his reappearance, the young man told reporters, "There's one thing that really bothers me. I have fiery red hair. Where was I that despite all the publicity no one recognized me?"

Seven days before Burkan's still unexplained disappearance, a thirty-seven-year -old research scientist named Paul T. MacGregor left his office at the Polaroid Corporation in Boston, Massachusetts, and started out for Camp Kirby to join his vacationing family. He never got there. One month later he walked into a police station in Buffalo, New York, and told them he didn't know who he was. His identity was traced through the labels of his clothes and the inscription on his wedding ring. Doctors at the Meyer Memorial Hospital examined him and said they were convinced that he was suffering from amnesia.

What traumatic event happened to these men to induce amnesia? Every year the media reports on cases where people appear with no memory of who they are and where they come from. Often when their identities are discovered, the amnesia victim is found to have been missing for months and even years, and hundreds of miles away from where they were last seen. A Londoner suddenly finds himself in South Africa. A girl from Cleveland awakes to discover she is in Australia. An unemployed Swedish milkman suddenly finds himself on a golf course on a remote island resort for the very rich. None of these people had any idea how they ended up so far away from home.

Time Travel – Fact Not Fiction

Mysterious disappearances, out of place objects, sightings of people, buildings, even entire towns that seem to be "unstuck in time." All of these things show that time is not entirely moving in a straight line to the future.

Time Travel – Fact Not Fiction

The Disappearance Of Danya

In the book *The Haunted Universe*, author D. Scott Rogo writes: "Needless to say, the casual reader may not be too impressed by these incidents of mysterious disappearances. I might add that until 1970, neither was I. Like so many others, it was easy for me to sit back complacently, assuring myself that eventually a normal explanation would be found for those inexplicable occurrences."

What changed Rogo's mind about strange disappearances concerned a woman named Danya. Rogo writes that she was a rather pathetic young girl whose basic pastimes were shacking up with men, partying and occasionally shooting up with drugs. Rogo got to know Danya in 1970 when she was befriended by an acquaintance-named Mark. They spent several weeks together in a little house situated behind some trees on a large lot on the outskirts of Los Angeles.

One night in August 1970, Danya went out to a party, leaving a group of friends behind at Mark's house. She returned at 12:15 AM. People in the house heard a car door slam out in the street, and looking out from behind the curtains, saw Danya's dim outline walking toward them. They sat back to wait for her arrival, but she never arrived. She had simply vanished at some point during the 150-foot walk from the street to the house.

Normal explanations for her disappearance seemed unlikely. Although her outline was dim, she was clearly recognized by those in the house. When the people who drove her home were contacted, they testified that they had dropped her off in front of the house and watched as she walked toward it before driving off. She left her belongings at the house and deserted her best friend and traveling companion who was also staying at the house.

What happens to people such as Danya? Obviously, they went somewhere. But since they were never seen again, we can at least tentatively conclude that, if in fact their disappearances were unnatural, they somehow entered or were transported into another Time and Space. Is this what happens to the hundreds of people who mysteriously disappear every year? Could these people be victims of some kind of "skip" or hole in time? If this is the case, are there any reports of their reappearance?

The Reappearing Groom

Writer John Macklin in his book *Orbits of the Unknown*, related the strange story of Father Litvinov, who just before midnight one evening in 1933, opened the church door to admit a young man in ornate knee breeches and a look of terror on his face.

Once the priest managed to calm the hysteria that had begun to seize his visitor, he heard an incredible story. The young man gave the name of Dmitri Girshkov, and he claimed that he was to have been married that day.

On his way to the church, he had stopped by the cemetery to visit the grave of a boyhood friend. As he had stood there paying his respects, he was startled to see what appeared to be the ghost of his dead friend. Dimitri said that it felt like he was in a dream. He could no longer hear the birds singing or the breeze blowing across the nearby tombstones. Then just as unexpectedly as he appeared, the apparition of his friend vanished into thin air. Suddenly, Dmitri realized it was dark outside, and as he made his way back to the village, he was shocked to find that nearly everything had changed in the small Siberian town.

Dmitri, after finishing his strange tale, ran from the church shouting in anguish that he must find his family, his friends, his bride. Chasing after his unusual guest, Father Litvinov went outside where he became aware of a strange light and a gray mist that surrounded the church. In the blinking of an eye, the young man had vanished into the night as quickly as he had appeared.

Intrigued by his experience, the priest went back through old parish records. Litvinov discovered that over the last two centuries, two other priests and a schoolmaster had seen the very same boy, who apparently, had stepped out of the past and into the future.

Finally, Litvinov found the name of Dmitri Girshkov and the records of a young man who, in 1746, on his wedding day, had went to visit the grave of a friend and disappeared. What had happened to Dmitri Girshkov? Did this unfortunate soul encounter a hole in time and space, finding himself being bounced along through the ages? If this was the case, what then was his ultimate fate? No one can say for sure. However, there have been no other recorded sightings since 1933 of the unfortunate groom lost in time.

Disappearances Into Time and Space

The May 4, 1958 issue of the *National Enquirer*, published a letter by a Mrs. G.H. Wales of Brooklyn, New York. In the letter, Mrs. Wales tells how in 1955 her husband had disappeared in front of her eyes as he climbed up to repair a clothesline pole. Mrs. Wales also noted in her

Time Travel – Fact Not Fiction

letter that her first husband had also disappeared in some mysterious fashion years before.

Charles Fort wrote about a strange incident in his book **LO**, that almost led to the disappearance of two children. On December 31, 1842, two young girls were gathering leaves from the ground near Clavaux, France. Stones began to fall around them with extreme slowness. The girls ran home and got their parents. When the girls returned to the spot, the stones started to fall once again. Then an upward current began to drag the girls upwards. The parents, who were not affected, grabbed their children's feet and managed to pull them to safety before they were out of reach.

A French-Canadian, Jean Durant, was apparently able to step in and out of time at will, until one day in 1898, when he lost control of his power and was never seen again. This case was brought to light by Nandor Fodor in the December 1956 issue of *Fate* magazine.

The article states that Durant's claim was tested by three doctors. They put him in one locked room where he disappeared and appeared in another. During one test, Durant was locked in a cell and chained to a wall and handcuffed. The cell door was then locked and sealed with wax at several spots. Durant passed the test and appeared among the startled watchers. The handcuffs were still locked and lay on the floor. The wax seals on the door were still intact.

One man named Williams, in a sworn written statement, stated he once saw Durant fade into nothing and his dressing gown fall to the ground once Durant had vanished.

It was Durant's demonstration in Chicago that did not go as expected. Durant's arms and legs were tied and the door was locked. When Durant didn't appear after an hour, the doctors entered the cell and found it empty. The handcuffs and rope were on the floor. That was the last time anyone saw Jean Durant. He had disappeared forever into the mists of time.

Two Strange Tales From Somerset

In 1768, a retired tailor named Owen Parfitt, disappeared from his home outside the village of Shepton Mallet, Somerset, England. Due to a stroke and arthritis, Parfitt was confined to a wheelchair as both his legs were paralyzed. He was taken care of by his sister and their 25-year-old maidservant Susannah Snook.

On the evening of Monday, June 6, 1768, Susannah Snook and Miss Parfitt had taken Owen out into the garden. Susannah had gone

Time Travel – Fact Not Fiction

back inside when Parfitt asked his sister to get him a scarf because it was getting chilly. She went in the house and returned in a few minutes but there was no sign of her brother. His wheelchair, pipe and the blanket which had covered his legs were still in the same spot.

The two women searched the area, but Owen was nowhere to be seen. By this time people had gathered to find out what had happened and helped in trying to find the old man. The search continued for the rest of the evening and through the night, despite the fact that about one hour afterwards, a storm blew up.

Nothing that might serve as a clue to the whereabouts of Owen Parfitt was found. He had vanished completely. One witness to the scene, Jehosaphat Stone, asserted that: "Many folk round here at the time believed that Owen Parfitt had been spirited off by supernatural means." This explanation is as good as any other. Parfitt was too poor to be worth robbing, so there was no suspicion of foul play and the case remains unsolved.

The second Somerset disappearance was written about by Rodney Davies in his book *Supernatural Vanishings*. Davies uncovered the fascinating story of Peter Williamson who mysteriously vanished, apparently after being struck by lighting.

On the evening of July 28, 1974, Peter Williamson, his wife Mary and their two children gave a barbecue at their house for a group of friends. The weather and been uncomfortably warm and humid all day, and as people arrived at the Williamson house, the sky was turning dark with storm clouds. The rain and lightning did not stop the party, as they were safe and dry under a covered porch.

It was not long afterwards that one of the Williamson's children noticed the family's dog was cowering under a bush on the opposite side of the lawn. Peter ran out into the rain to rescue the dog when, suddenly, a huge flash of lightning struck a nearby tree. Peter seemed to be strangely illuminated by the lightning's flash. Unexpectedly, in front of the entire group of people, Peter vanished from sight.

His wife Mary and the children screamed, and the others ran out into the rain to see what had happened. But despite their frantic search, which took them all over the high-walled garden, they found no sign of Peter Williamson.

The police were called in and the area around the house was searched for any evidence to shed light on what had happened to Williamson. Three days later, the Williamson's gardener found his missing employer lying semiconscious in some shrubbery at the end of the garden. The returned Peter Williamson was completely unharmed, yet strangely, was dressed somewhat differently from when he had vanished. Williamson was taken to a local hospital, where it was determined that apart from being in a state of shock, he was suffering from nothing worse than amnesia. Frustratingly for all concerned, Peter could remember nothing of what had happened to him.

After a brief stay in the hospital, Williamson went home to fully recuperate. Peter soon began to have a series of disjointed graphic dreams that seemed to show what had happened to him during those lost sixty hours.

In his dreams, Peter found himself coming to in another garden, his clothes soaked through, but without knowing where he was or how he got there. Close by the garden, Peter noticed there was a narrow road and he staggered to his feet and went to it. He walked along the road for some distance until he began to feel so weak and ill that he sat down along the side to rest.

Fortunately, a passing motorist, who happened to be a doctor, stopped and offered assistance. When the doctor learned Peter had lost his memory, he drove him to a hospital. There, Peter was admitted, but he was completely unable to tell the staff his name or address, and as he carried no identification nothing could be learned about him or his situation. The doctors were baffled by his condition, but told Peter he might regain his memory in a few days.

In his dreams, Peter remembered that the ward in which he was placed seemed to shimmer eerily and that his doctor's name was Nugent, and the ward's sister's name was Alice Charles. He also recalled that his voice was slurred and unusually slow, compared with the brisk, clear tones of the doctor and nurses.

Peter dreamed that on the second day at the hospital when he felt better, he told the nurse in charge that he wanted to get up and take a short walk. He was told, however, that his jeans had been thrown away because they were stained and torn.

The man in the next bed, hearing Peter's plight offered to loan Peter a pair of brown corduroy trousers. He gratefully accepted them, slipped on the rest of his clothes and walked down to the hospital cafe. On the third day, Peter took a longer walk and found the road that led back to the garden where he had first awakened. This is where his dreams would end, giving no clue how he ended up back in his own yard.

Peter soon realized that his dreams might be actual repressed memories of his three-day ordeal. This was confirmed when he found the brown corduroy trousers, which had been loaned to him by the man in his dream, hanging in his closet where they had been placed by his wife. He knew that if he could trace the owner, he would be able to both return them and find out where the strange hospital was found.

He could see that the pants were new, and from the label, he found that they had been made by Herbert Cox, a West Country manufacturer, they also bore the owners initials "J.B." monogrammed onto the label. Yet, when he tried to locate the manufacturer, he was dismayed to discover that they had been out of business since 1954.

Sometime later, Peter went to the local hospital for a checkup, and by chance overheard a "Dr. Nugent" being mentioned. He asked where he might find that physician, and was told that Dr. Nugent was employed at the cottage hospital that stood, not more than a half a mile from his own home. Peter had not known of this hospital's existence, yet it seemed obvious that it must be where the doctor had taken him.

On leaving the local hospital, he went straight to the cottage hospital, which he recognized from his dreams. When Peter finally met Dr. Nugent, he was surprised that the Doctor seemed older than he remembered. Where his hair had been dark, his temples were now thinning and gray.

Dr. Nugent did not return Peter's welcoming smile with the burst of recognition that he had expected. In fact, the man did not seem to recognize him at all. Mystified, Peter introduced himself and explained that he was the amnesia victim that Dr. Nugent had recently treated.

The physician looked hard at him, shook his head, and said to Peter, "I'm afraid you have the wrong hospital old chap. I've never seen you before, and I haven't had an amnesia case for a number of years."

What can we make from this case? Did Peter Williamson suffer from amnesia and wander the countryside in a daze for three days until, somehow, he found his way back home again? Or, more incredibly, had Peter been thrown out of his time and into the past by the blast of lightning?

Other cases of temporal displacement appear to be initiated by some form of outside catalyst, say a close lightning strike. However, just as often, there appears to be no discernible reason why the displacement should occur in the first place. There are no easy answers to these questions, or even if the right questions have been asked. However, proof does remain with the Williamson case in the

Time Travel – Fact Not Fiction

form of a pair of brown pants loaned to Peter by a friendly stranger from some other place and time.

The Disaster Ladder

The book **ESP Forewarnings** by Robert Tralins contains a story of the weird disappearance of Ludwig Massey. Massey, a warehouse clerk living in Cincinnati, Ohio, had a fear of ladders. Massey felt that a "disaster ladder" would one day cause his death. He could offer no rational explanation for his feelings; he just insisted that he knew that one day he would die because of a ladder.

Massey had several unfortunate accidents after going under ladders. In June 1966, while at work, Massey walked under a ladder while taking inventory. One employee swears he saw Massey vanish into thin air. An immediate search failed to locate Massey. Like others before him, Ludwig Massey was never seen again.

The Strange Disappearance Of Captain Franklin Briggs

According to the December 10, 1955 issue of the **Navy Times**, written by Michael MacDougall, strange disappearances may not be entirely random events. MacDougall writes, "We were gathered in the lobby of the Nordale Hotel in Fairbanks, Alaska waiting for the airport limousine. From the doorway, I could see the bank on the corner. Instead of the customary clock, a huge temperature indicator was suspended over the door. The sign read 45 degrees below zero.

"'That means it's sixty below in the back country,' said one of the travelers. 'I sure pity those poor devils.'

"He was referring to an unsolved mystery we had just been discussing. Three hunters and flown to a spot close by the Arctic Circle. A week later, Eskimos had found the plane, well secured and fully stocked with equipment and provisions, but the men had vanished. The wife of one of the missing men was seated in a corner, twisting and untwisting her hands. She could remember nothing about what had happened to her, or the fate of her husband and his companions.

"'She should go back to the States,' said an outbound passenger. 'They'll never find her husband.'

"'What makes you so sure?' I asked.

"'His name is Franklin Briggs. He's a Navy captain. His father, Major Briggs, was reported missing in action in World War 1. His grandfather, another Captain Briggs, was listed as missing in Cuba in

1898. He never turned up either. And that's not all. His great-grandfather was the famous Captain Benjamin Briggs.'

"'Captain Briggs,' I repeated. 'Why was he famous?'

"'He was the skipper of the Mary Celeste, the ship that lost her crew on the voyage from New York to Genoa in 1872, the most baffling mystery of the sea ever. A drifting derelict off the Azores, why had a seaworthy ship been deserted by all aboard? Lloyd's of London, who carried the insurance, sent investigators into every port in the world. Not a trace has ever been found of the crew or officers. There have been dozens of fantastic theories, but no hard facts. The mystery of the Mary Celeste is still a mystery.'

"He paused, and then continued. 'That's why I say Mrs. Briggs should return to the States. They'll never find her husband just as they never found any of the other Briggs.' And true to his word, Captain Franklin Briggs was never found."

Teleportation Or Lost In Time And Space?

The following story comes from the publication of the now defunct Shaver Mystery Club. While exact details such as names and dates have not been included, it is thought by many investigators that this story is true. In California, a band was playing at a mansion of a local citrus baron. At the end of the party, the band carried out their instruments. The drummer walked through a pair of French doors and, carrying his bass drum, wandered off through the surrounding orange orchard.

That was the last that anyone, so far as is known, has ever seen of the man. He left a wife and family, social position, good living and just vanished. Authorities and private investigators could uncover no clues as to his whereabouts, nor the means by which he disappeared. Apparently, he entered the orchard, dressed in black evening wear, carrying a bass drum on his back, and never reappeared.

Years later, someone reading a copy of one of Charles Fort's books found an account of an Australian party encamped in the vast desert of the interior of that continent. Into the light of their campfire, about which the party was gathered, strode a white man, immaculately clad in evening clothes, and carrying a bass drum on his back. He seemed not to be dusty or tired. He showed no evidence of having walked more than a few yards through the wilderness of the Australian bush. The stranger could not tell how he happened to get there, how he arrived, nor did he know his own identity. He returned to civilization with the party and Fort states his identity was never established.

A case recorded by writer Brad Steiger involves a veteran of World War II who told of walking up an Italian street one night shortly after the Allied occupation, heard a slight buzzing sound above him, and the next thing he knew he was in northern France. Four months had elapsed, but to him only a second had passed. Seemingly, as a compensation for this loss of time he was given powers of clairvoyance.

"He lives today," writes Steiger, "in a Midwestern city, more disturbed than elated by his gift from unknown donors."

Two brothers named Pansini, seven and eight years old had a strange run-in with time and space in 1910. At 9PM they were in Ruvo, Italy. Half an hour later, they were found wandering dazedly in the gardens of the Capuchin convent in Malfatti, 30 miles away. How had they been transported that distance so quickly? The two boys could offer no explanation. They told authorities that they had been playing outside when they were suddenly surrounded by a thick gray mist. The next thing they knew they found themselves in the convent's garden. Such a thing could happen very easily nowadays with cars, but in 1901 it was a miraculous event.

Elevator Ride To Nowhere

In the September 1956 issue of *Fate* magazine, Miriam Golding wrote about her unusual experience that occurred in the fall of 1934 when she stepped out of an elevator and became unstuck in time.

Miriam and her fiancé were riding a crowded elevator in a Chicago music store when she got off on the wrong floor and found it impossible to get back on the crowded elevator. After the elevator containing her fiancé left, Miriam looked around her and was startled to see that she was not in a downtown building at all, but in a large railroad station.

She watched crowds of travelers hurrying about. Railroad announcers gave times of departures and arrivals and Miriam could hear the sounds of train engines as they arrived and left the terminal. Miriam approached the Information Booth, but was completely ignored by the girl behind the counter. It was as if Miriam was invisible to everyone around her.

At last Miriam noticed a to-the-street sign and followed it into the open air. It seemed to be a beautiful, midsummer afternoon. A new, red brick building was being built across the street from the station. Crowds of people walked by on the streets. But everyone ignored Miriam as she tried to ask for directions.

She wandered aimlessly for several minutes until she noticed a teenage boy standing near the center of the sidewalk, staring in all directions. She approached the boy, hardly daring to hope that he might see her. Then he noticed her and smiled: "I guess they let you off at the wrong stop too!"

Miriam immediately understood that. "However fantastic, the same thing had happened to both of us. Our mutual plight created a bond and for want of anything better to do, we continued together down the street." The boy explained that he had been playing tennis in Lincoln, Nebraska. He had gone into the locker room to change his shoes, and when he came out, he found himself inexplicably in the same train depot.

Eventually they found themselves in the open country where, Miriam saw her fiancé's sister with a number of other girls on a sandbar in the middle of a river. They noticed her too and began to call her name and wave at her.

Her new friend became very excited. Perhaps the girls formed some kind of connection or link between times. "It's not far to swim," he told Miriam. "They see us; I know I can make it to them in a few minutes."

The figures of the girls remained on the sandbar, but the teenager, even though he was a strong swimmer, could not reach the sandbar. Exhausted, he returned to shore and fell to the ground in discouragement. When they looked again at the sandbar, it, along with the girls, had disappeared.

Miriam felt despondent. Would she be forever trapped in this other time? Then she became suddenly enveloped in darkness. She felt as if she were floating through space.

Suddenly she found herself on a stool in the music store, a magazine spread out before her. A clock was signaling closing time. Miriam looked around for her fiancé, but she could not see him. She decided to go to his house.

"When I got to my destination," Miriam Golding wrote, "my fiancé opened the door. He certainly looked relieved. He said he'd lost me on the elevator. After stepping out on the main floor, he had been unable to locate me. Thinking I had gotten off on some other floor, he had waited a while, decided to go home." Miriam entered the home

Time Travel – Fact Not Fiction

and was surprised to see her fiancé's sister with the same friends she had seen on the sandbar. The sister smiled and said that she had seen Miriam in town, "but you were so engrossed in each other you didn't even hear us."

Miriam Golding was one of the lucky ones. For some unknown reason she found herself lost in time. However, unlike others who have probably found themselves in similar situations, Miriam was somehow able to return to her own time and place. Some questions remain though. What happened to the teenager that accompanied Miriam? Why had her fiancé's sister seen her with her fiancé instead of the teenager?

These cases seem to show that our knowledge of the workings of time is simply inadequate. Rather than being caged in by the so-called "forward" movement of time, some people have discovered that there are shortcuts back and forth across the stream of time. This appears to be a natural occurrence. When the conditions are right, holes in the fabric of Time/Space open and if someone is unfortunate enough to be nearby when this happens, they can fall in, perhaps never to return. However, there are cases where the barriers of time fall away for a while giving a glimpse of what once was.

Chapter Three
The Adventure: A Journey Through Time?

First published in 1911, **The Adventure** tells about an extraordinary encounter of two scholarly English women, the Principal and Vice-principal of St. Hugh's College at Oxford, while walking in the Petit Trianon Gardens at Versailles in 1901 France.

The two women suddenly found themselves allegedly in a scene from 1789 and encountered many characters, one who may have been Marie-Antoinette. What sets this account above other similar tales is the impeccable character of the two women, the vivid independent accounts and intricate descriptions given by each, and the painstaking research and documentation over many years undertaken by them.

Their attention to every detail and discoveries of facts supporting their account, some not known until years after the event, makes this a most absorbing story.

Miss Moberly's Account Of The First Visit to
The Petit Trianon

August 1901: After some days of sightseeing in Paris, to which we were almost strangers, on an August afternoon, 1901, Miss Jourdain and I went to Versailles. We had very hazy ideas as to where it was or what there was to be seen. Both of us thought it might prove to be a dull expedition.

We went by train, and walked through the rooms and galleries of the Palace with interest, though we constantly regretted our inability through ignorance to feel properly the charm of the place. My knowledge of French history was limited to the very little I had learnt in the schoolroom, historical novels, and the first volume of Justin McCarthy's French Revolution.

Over thirty years before my brother had written a prize poem on Marie Antoinette, for whom at the time I had felt much enthusiasm. But the German occupation was chiefly in our minds, and Miss Jourdain and I thought and spoke of it several times. We sat in the Salle des Glaces, where a very sweet air was blowing in at the open windows

Time Travel – Fact Not Fiction

over the flowerbeds below, and finding that there was time to spare, I suggested our going to the Petit Trianon. My sole knowledge of it was from a magazine article read as a girl, from which I received a general impression that it was a farmhouse where the Queen had amused herself. Looking in Baedeker's map we saw the sort of direction and that there were two Trianons, and set off.

By not asking the way, we went an unnecessarily long way round—by the great flights of steps from the fountains and down the central avenue as far as the head of the long pond. The weather had been very hot all the week, but on this day, the sky was a little overcast and the sun shaded. There was a lively wind blowing, the woods were looking their best, and we both felt particularly vigorous. It was a most enjoyable walk.

After reaching the beginning of the long water, we struck away to the right down a woodland glade until we came obliquely to the other water close to the building which we rightly concluded to be the Grand Trianon. We passed it on our left hand, and came upon a broad green drive perfectly deserted. If we had followed it we should have come immediately to the Petit Trianon, but, not knowing its position, we crossed the drive and went up a lane in front of us.

I was surprised that Miss Jourdain did not ask the way from a woman who was shaking a white cloth out of the window of a building at the corner of the lane, but followed, supposing that she knew where she was going to. Talking about England, and mutual acquaintances there, we went up the lane, and then made a sharp turn to the right past some buildings. We looked in at an open doorway and saw the end of a carved staircase, but as no one was about we did not like to go in.

There were three paths in front of us, and as we saw two men a little ahead on the center one, we followed it, and asked them the way. Afterwards we spoke of them as gardeners, because we remembered a wheelbarrow of some kind close by and the look of a pointed spade, but they were really very dignified officials, dressed in long greyish-green coats with small three-cornered hats. They without saying a single word to us, they directed us straight on with gestures of their hands.

We walked briskly forward, talking as before, but from the moment we left the lane an extraordinary depression had come over me, which, in spite of every effort to shake off, steadily deepened. There seemed to be absolutely no reason for it; I was not at all tired, and was becoming more interested in my surroundings. I was anxious that my companion should not discover the sudden gloom upon my spirits, which became quite overpowering on reaching the point where the path ended, being crossed by another, right and left.

In front of us was a wood, within which, and overshadowed by trees, was a light garden kiosk, circular, and like a small bandstand, by which a man was sitting. There was no greensward, but the ground was covered with rough grass and dead leaves as in a wood. The place was so shut in that we could not see beyond it. Everything suddenly looked unnatural, therefore unpleasant; even the trees behind the building seemed to have become flat and lifeless, like a wood worked in tapestry. There were no effects of light and shade, and no wind stirred the trees. It was all intensely still.

The man sitting close to the kiosk (who had on a cloak and a large shady hat) turned his head and looked at us. That was the culmination of my peculiar sensations, and I felt a moment of genuine alarm. The man's face was most repulsive—his expression odious. His complexion was very dark and rough. I said to Miss Jourdain, "Which is our way?" But thought: "nothing will induce me to go to the left."

It was a great relief at that moment to hear someone running up to us in breathless haste. Connecting the sound with the gardeners, I turned and ascertained that there was no one on the paths, either to the side or behind, but at almost the same moment I suddenly perceived another man quite close to us, behind and rather to the left hand, who had, apparently, just come either over or through the rock (or whatever it was) that shut out the view at the junction of the paths. The suddenness of his appearance was something of a shock.

The second man was distinctly a gentleman; he was tall, with large dark eyes, and had crisp, curling black hair under the same large sombrero hat. He was handsome, and the effect of the hair was to make him look like an old picture. His face was glowing red as through great exertion—as though he had come a long way.

At first I thought he was sunburnt, but a second look satisfied me that the color was from heat, not sunburning. He had on a dark cloak wrapped across him like a scarf, one end flying out in his prodigious hurry. He looked greatly excited as he called out to us, "Mesdames, Mesdames" (or Madame' pronounced more as the other), "il ne faut (pronounced fout) 'pas passer par là." He then waved his arm, and said with great animation, "par ici...cherchez la maison."

I was so surprised at his eagerness that I looked up at him again, and to this he responded with a little backward movement and a most peculiar smile. Though I could not follow all he said, it was clear that he was determined that we should go to the right and not to the

Time Travel – Fact Not Fiction

left. As this fell in with my own wish, I went instantly toward a little bridge on the right, and turning my head to join Miss Jourdain in thanking him, found, to my surprise, that he was not there, but the running began again, and from the sound it was close beside us.

Silently we passed over the small rustic bridge, which crossed a tiny ravine. So close to us when on the bridge that we could have touched it with our right hands, a threadlike cascade fell from a height down a green pretty bank, where ferns grew between stones. Where the little trickle of water went to I did not see, but it gave me the impression that we were near other water, though I saw none.

Beyond the little bridge our pathway led under trees; it skirted a narrow meadow of long grass, bounded on the farther side by trees, and very much overshadowed by trees growing in it. This gave the whole place a somber look suggestive of dampness, and shut out the view of the house until we were close to it.

The house was a square, solidly built small country house—quite different from what I expected. The long windows looking north into the English garden (where we were) were shuttered. There was a terrace round the north and west sides of the house, and on the rough grass, which grew quite up to the terrace, and with her back to it, a lady was sitting, holding out a paper as though to look at it at arms' length. I supposed her to be sketching, and to have brought her own campstool.

It seemed as though she must be making a study of trees, for they grew close in front of her, and there seemed to be nothing else to sketch. She saw us, and when we passed close by on her left hand, she turned and looked full at us. It was not a young face, and (though rather pretty) it did not attract me. She had on a shady white hat perched on a good deal of fair hair that fluffed round her forehead. Her light summer dress was arranged on her shoulders in handkerchief fashion, and there was a little line of either green or gold near the edge of the handkerchief, which showed me that it was over, not tucked into, her bodice, which was cut low. Her dress was long-waisted, with a good deal of fullness in the skirt, which seemed to be short.

I thought she was a tourist, but that her dress was old-fashioned and rather unusual (though people were wearing fichu bodices that summer). I looked straight at her; but some indescribable feeling made me turn away annoyed at her being there.

We went up the steps onto the terrace, my impression being that they led up direct from the English garden; but I was beginning to

Time Travel – Fact Not Fiction

feel as though we were walking in a dream—the stillness and oppressiveness were so unnatural.

Again, I saw the lady, this time from behind, and noticed that her fichu was pale green. It was rather a relief to me that Miss Jourdain did not propose to ask her whether we could enter the house from that side.

We crossed the terrace to the southwest corner and looked over into the cour d'honneur; and then turned back, and seeing that one of the long windows overlooking the French garden was unshuttered, we were going toward it when we were interrupted. The terrace was prolonged at right angles in front of what seemed to be a second house.

The door of it suddenly opened, and a young man stepped out onto the terrace, banging the door behind him. He had the jaunty manner of a footman, but no livery, and called to us, saying that the way into the house was by the cour d'honneur, and offered to show us the way round. He looked inquisitively amused as he walked by us down the French garden till we came to an entrance into the front drive. We came out sufficiently near the first lane we had been in to make me wonder why the garden officials had not directed us back instead of telling us to go forward.

When we were in the front entrance hall, we were kept waiting for the arrival of a merry French wedding-party. They walked arm-in-arm in a long procession round the rooms, and we were at the back—too far off from the guide to hear much of his story. We were very much interested, and felt quite lively again.

Coming out of the cour d'honneur we took a little carriage which was standing there, and drove back to the Hôtel des Réservoirs, in Versailles, where we had tea; but we were neither of us inclined to talk, and did not mention any of the events of the afternoon. After the tea, we walked back to the station, looking on the way for the Tennis Court.

On the way back to Paris the setting sun at last burst out from under the clouds, bathing the distant Versailles woods in glowing light—Valerien standing out in front a mass of deep purple. Again and again the thought returned—"Was Marie Antoinette really much at Trianon, and did she see it for the last time long before the fatal drive to Paris accompanied by the mob?"

For a whole week we never alluded to that afternoon, nor did I think about it until I began writing a descriptive letter of our expeditions of the week before. As the scenes came back, one by one, the same sensation of dreamy unnatural oppression came over me so strongly that I stopped writing, and said to Miss Jourdain, "Do you think that the Petit Trianon is haunted?" Her answer was prompt, "Yes I do." I asked her where she felt it, and she said, "In the garden where we met the two men, but not only there."

She then described her feeling of depression and anxiety which began at the same point as it did with me, and how she tried not to let me know it. Talking it over we fully realized, for the first time, the theatrical appearance of the man who spoke to us, the inappropriateness of the wrapped cloak on a warm summer afternoon, the unaccountableness of his coming and going, the excited running which seemed to begin and end close to us, and yet always out of sight, and the extreme earnestness with which he desired us to go one way and not another.

I said that the thought had crossed my mind that the two men were going to fight a duel, and that they were waiting until we were gone. Miss Jourdain owned to having disliked the thought of passing the man of the kiosk. We did not speak again of the incident during my stay in Paris. We visited the Conciergerie prisons, and the tombs of Louis XVI and Marie Antoinette at Saint-Denis, where all was fresh and natural and nothing seemed out of the ordinary.

Three months later Miss Jourdain came to stay with me, and on Sunday, 10th November, 1901, we returned to the subject, and I said, "If we had known that a lady was sitting so near us sketching it would have made all the difference, for we should have asked the way." She replied that she had seen no lady. I found this strange, so I reminded her of the person sitting under the terrace, but Miss Jourdain declared that there was no one there.

I exclaimed that it was impossible that she should not have seen the individual for we were walking side by side and went straight up to her, passed her and looked down upon her from the terrace. It was inconceivable to us both that she should not have seen the lady, but the fact was clear that Miss Jourdain had not done so, though we had both been rather on the lookout for someone who would reassure us as to whether we were trespassing or not.

Finding that we had a new element of mystery, and doubting how far we had seen any of the same things, we resolved to write down independent accounts of our expedition to Trianon, read up its history, and make every inquiry about the place. Miss Jourdain returned to her school the same evening, and I eagerly awaited her response. Finally, two days later I received from her a very interesting letter, giving the result of her first inquiries.

Time Travel – Fact Not Fiction

Miss Jourdain's Account Of Her Visit To The Petit Trianon

August 1901:   In the summer of 1900 I stayed in Paris for the first time, and in the course of that summer took a flat and furnished it, intending to place a French lady there in charge of my elder schoolgirls. Paris was quite new to me, and beyond seeing the picture galleries and one or two churches, I made no expeditions except to shops, for the Exhibition of 1900 was going on, and all my free time was spent in seeing it with my French friends.

The next summer, however, 1901, when, after several months at my school in England, I came back to Paris, it was to take the first opportunity possible of having a visitor to stay there: and I asked Miss Moberly to come with me.   Miss Moberly suggested our seeing the historic part of Paris in something like chronological order, and I looked forward to seeing it practically for the first time with her.

We decided to go to Versailles one day, though rather reluctantly, as we felt it was diverging from our plan to go there too soon. I did not know what to expect, as my ignorance of the place and its significance was extreme. So we looked up general directions in Baedeker, and trusted to finding our way at the time even though we were not familiar with the area and knew that we risked getting ourselves lost.

After spending some time in the Palace, we went down by the terrace and struck to the right to find the Petit Trianon. We walked for some distance down a wooded alley, and then came upon the buildings of the Grand Trianon, before which we did not delay.

We went on in the direction of the Petit Trianon, but just before reaching what we knew afterwards to be the main entrance I saw a gate leading to a path cut deep below the level of the ground above, and as the way was open and had the look of an entrance that was used, I said, "Shall we try this path? It must lead to the house," and we followed it. To our right we saw some farm-buildings looking empty and deserted; implements (among others a plough) were lying about; we looked in, but saw no one. The impression was saddening, but it was not until we reached the crest of the rising ground where there was a garden that I began to feel as if we had lost our way, and as if something was wrong.

There were two men there in official dress (greenish in color), with something in their hands; it might have been a staff. A wheelbarrow and some other gardening tools were near them. They told us, in answer to my enquiry, to go straight on. I remember repeating my question, because they answered in a seemingly casual and mechanical way, but only got the same answer in the same manner.

As we were standing there, I saw to the right of us a detached solidly built cottage, with stone steps at the door. A woman and a girl were standing at the doorway, and I particularly noticed their unusual dress; both wore white kerchiefs tucked into the bodice, and the girl's dress, though she looked thirteen or fourteen only, was down to her ankles. The woman was passing a jug to the girl, who wore a close white cap. Following the directions of the two men we walked on: but the path pointed out to us seemed to lead away from where we imagined the Petit Trianon to be; and there was a feeling of depression and loneliness about the place.

I began to feel as if I were walking in my sleep; the heavy dreaminess was oppressive. At last we came upon a path crossing ours, and saw in front of us a building consisting of some columns roofed in, and set back in the trees. Seated on the steps was a man with a heavy black cloak round his shoulders, and wearing a slouch hat. At that moment the eerie feeling which had begun in the garden culminated in a definite impression of something uncanny and fear-inspiring.

The man slowly turned his face, which was marked by smallpox: his complexion was very dark. The expression was very evil and yet unseeing, and though I did not feel that he was looking particularly at us, I felt a repugnance to going past him. But I did not wish to show the feeling, which I thought was meaningless, and we talked about the best way to turn, and decided to go to the right.

Suddenly we heard a man running behind us: he shouted, "Mesdames, mesdames," and when I turned he said in an accent that seemed to me unusual that our way lay in another direction. "Il ne faut (pronounced fout) `pas passer par là." He then made a gesture, adding, "par ici...cherchez la maison."

Though we were surprised to be addressed, we were glad of the direction, and I thanked him. The man ran off with a curious smile on his face: the running ceased as abruptly as it had begun, not far from where we stood. I remember that the man was young-looking, with a florid complexion and rather long dark hair. I do not remember the dress, except that the material was dark and heavy, and that the man wore buckled shoes.

We walked on, crossing a small bridge that went across a green bank, high on our right hand and shelving down below as to a very small overshadowed pool of water glimmering some way off. A tiny stream descended from above us, so small as to seem to lose itself before reaching the little pool. We then followed a narrow path till almost immediately we came upon the English garden front of the Petit Trianon. The place was deserted; but as we approached the terrace I remember drawing my skirt away with a feeling as though someone were near and I had to make room, and then wondering why I did it. While we were on the terrace a boy came out of the door of a second building which opened on it, and I still have the sound in my ears of his slamming it behind him.

He directed us to go round to the other entrance, and, seeing us hesitate, with the peculiar smile of suppressed mockery offered to show us the way. We passed through the French garden, part of which was walled in by trees. The feeling of dreariness was very strong there, and continued till we actually reached the front entrance to the Petit Trianon and looked round the rooms in the wake of a French wedding-party. Afterwards we drove back to the Rue des Réservoirs without speaking of our unusual day.

The impression returned to me at intervals during the week that followed, but I did not speak of it until Miss Moberly asked me if I thought the Petit Trianon was haunted, and I said yes.

It was not till three months later, when I was staying with her, that Miss Moberly casually mentioned the lady, and almost refused to believe that I had not seen her. How that happened was quite inexplicable, to me, for I believed myself to be looking about on all sides, and it was not so much that I did not remember her as that I could have said no one was there. But as she said it I remembered my impression at the moment of there being more people than I could see, though I did not tell her this.

The same evening, November 10, 1901, I returned to my school near London. Curiously enough, the next morning I had to give one of a set of lessons on the French Revolution for the Higher Certificate, and it struck me for the first time with great interest that the 10th of August had a special significance in French history, and that we had been at Trianon on the anniversary of the day.

That evening, when I was preparing to write down my experiences, a French friend whose home was in Paris came into my room, and I asked her, just on the chance, if she knew any story about the haunting of the Petit Trianon. (I had not mentioned our story to her before, nor indeed to anyone.) She said directly that she remembered hearing from friends at Versailles that on a certain day in August Marie Antoinette is regularly seen sitting outside the garden front at the Petit Trianon, with a light flapping hat and a pink dress.

Above: Miss Anne Moberley (left) and Miss Eleanor Jourdain (right). After their visit to the Petit Trianon, Miss Moberley asked Miss Jourdain, "Do you think the Petit Trianon is haunted?" Miss Jourdain did.

Below: Petit Trianon, the small mansion built on the grounds of Versailles and once belonging to Marie-Antoinette.

Time Travel – Fact Not Fiction

More than this, that the place, especially the farm, the garden, and the path by the water, are peopled with those who used to be with her there; in fact that all the occupations and amusements reproduce themselves there for a day and a night. I then told her our story, and when I quoted the words that the man spoke to us, and imitated as well as I could his accent, she immediately said that it was the Austrian pronunciation of French. I had privately thought that he spoke old French, but I did not speak my mind out loud at the time. Immediately afterwards I wrote and told this to Miss Moberly.

Miss Moberly's Thoughts On What May Have Occurred

On receiving Miss Jourdain's letter I turned to my diary to see on what Saturday in August it was that we had visited Versailles, and looked up the history to find out to what event she alluded. On August 10, 1792, the Tuileries was sacked. The royal family escaped in the early morning to the Hall of the Assembly, where they were penned up for many hours hearing themselves practically deposed, and within sound of the massacre of their servants and of the Swiss Guards at the Tuileries. From the Hall the King and Queen were taken to the Temple.

We wondered whether we had inadvertently entered within an act of the Queen's memory when alive, and whether this explained our curious sensation of being completely shut in and oppressed. What more likely, we thought, than that during those hours in the Hall of the Assembly, or in the Conciergerie, she had gone back in time with such vivid memory to other Augusts spent at Trianon that some impression of it was imparted to the place.

Some pictures which were shown to me proved that the outdoor dress of the gentlemen at Court had been a large hat and cloak, and that the ladies wore long-waisted bodices, with full gathered short skirts, fichus, and hats. I told the story to my brother, and we heartily agreed that, as a rule, such stories made no impression at all upon us, because we always believed that, if only the persons involved would take the trouble to investigate them thoroughly and honestly for themselves, they could be quite naturally explained.

We agreed that such a story as ours had very little value without more proof of reality than it had, but that as there were one or two interesting points in it, it would be best to sift the matter quietly, lest others should make more of them than they deserved. He suggested lightly and in fun that perhaps we had seen the Queen as she thought of herself, and that it would be interesting to know whether the dress described was the one she had on at the time of her rêverie, or whether it was one she recollected having worn at an earlier date.

My brother also asked whether we were quite sure that the last man we had seen (who came out of the side building), as well as the wedding-party, were all real persons. I assured him with great amusement that we had not the smallest doubt as to the reality of them all.

As Miss Jourdain was going to Paris for the Christmas holidays, I wrote and asked her to take any opportunity she might have to see the place again, and to make a plan of the paths and the buildings; for the guidebooks spoke of the Temple de l'Amour and the Belvédère, and I thought one of them might prove to be our kiosk.

Miss Jourdain's Account Of Her Second Visit

January 1902: On January 2, 1902, I went for the second time to Versailles. It was a cold and wet day, but I was anxious not to be deterred by that, as it was likely to be my only possible day that winter. This time I drove straight to the Petit Trianon, passing the Grand Trianon. Here I could see the path up which we had walked in August.

I went, however, to the regular entrance, thinking I would go at once to the Temple de l'Amour, even if I had time to go no farther. To the right of the cour d'honneur was a door in the wall; it led to the Hameau de la Reine and to the gardens. I took this path and came to the Temple de l'Amour, which was not the building we had passed in the summer.

There was, so far, none of the eerie feeling we had experienced in August. But, on crossing a bridge to go to the Hameau, the old feeling returned in full force; it was as if I had crossed a line and was suddenly in a circle of influence. To the left I saw a tract of park-like ground, the trees bare and very scanty. I noticed a cart being filled with sticks by two laborers, and thought I could go to them for directions if I lost my way.

The men wore tunics and capes with pointed hoods of bright colors, a sort of terra cotta red and deep blue. I turned aside for an instant, not more, to look at the Hameau, and when I looked back men and cart were completely out of sight, and this surprised me, as I could see a long way in every direction. And though I had seen the men in the act of loading the cart with sticks, I could not see any trace of them on the ground, either at the time or afterwards. I did not, however, dwell upon any part of the incident, but went on to the Hameau. As I look back now on this incident it does seem strange to me that I failed to question the sudden disappearance of the men.

The houses were all built near a sheet of water, and the old oppressive feeling of the last year was noticeable, especially under the balcony of the Maison de la Reine, and near a window in what I afterwards found to be the Laiterie. I really felt a great reluctance to go near the window or look in, and when I did so I found it shuttered inside.

Coming away from the Hameau, I at last reached a building, which I knew from my plan to be the small Orangerie; then, meaning to go to the Belvédère, I turned back by mistake into the park and found myself in a wood so thick that though I had turned toward the Hameau, but I could not see it.

Before I entered, I looked across an open space toward a belt of trees to the left of the Hameau some way off, and noticed a man, cloaked like those we had seen before, slip swiftly through the line of trees. The smoothness of his movement attracted my attention.

I was puzzling my way among the mazes of paths in the wood when I heard a rustling behind me, which made me wonder why people in silk dresses came out on such a wet day. I said to myself, "just like French people." I turned sharply round to see who they were, but saw no one, and then, all in a moment, I had the same feeling as by the terrace in the summer, only in a much greater degree; it was as though I were closed in by a group of people who already filled the path, coming from behind and passing me.

At one moment, there seemed really no room for me. I heard some women's voices talking French, and caught the words "Monsieur et Madame" said close to my ear. The crowd got scarce and drifted away, and then faint music as of a band, not far off, was audible. It was playing very light music with a good deal of repetition in it. Both voices and music were diminished in tone, as in a phonograph, unnaturally. The pitch of the bank was lower than usual. The sounds were intermittent, and once more, I felt the swish of a dress close by me.

I looked at the map which I had with me, but whenever I settled which path to take I felt impelled to go by another. After turning backwards and forwards many times I at last found myself back at the Orangerie, and was overtaken by a gardener. I asked him where I should find the Queen's grotto that had been mentioned in De Nolhac's book, which I had procured while in Paris. He told me to

Time Travel – Fact Not Fiction

follow the path I was on, and, in answer to a question, said that I must pass the Belvédère, adding that it was quite impossible to find one's way about the park unless one had been brought up in the place and so used to it that "personne ne pourrait vous tromper."The expression specially impressed me because of the experience I had just had in the wood. He pointed out the way and left me. The path led past the Belvédère, which I took for granted was the building we had seen in August, for, coming upon it from behind, all the water was hidden from me. I made my way from there to the French garden without noticing the paths I took. On my return to Versailles I made careful inquiries as to whether the band had been playing there that day, but was told that though it was the usual day of the week, it had not played because it had played the day before, being New Year's Day.

I told my French friends of my walk, and they said that there was a tradition of Marie Antoinette having been seen making butter within the Laiterie, and for that reason it was shuttered. A second tradition they mentioned interested me very much. It was that on October 5, 1789—which was the last day on which Marie Antoinette went to Trianon—she was sitting in her grotto, and saw a page running toward her, bringing the letter from the minister at the Palace to say that the mob from Paris would be at the gates in an hour. The story went on that she impulsively proposed walking straight back to the Palace by the short cut through the trees. He would not allow it; but begged her to go to the `maison' to wait whilst he fetched the carriage by which she was generally conveyed back through the park, and that he ran off to order it.

Miss Moberly Investigates Their Adventure

During the next two years very little occurred to throw light on the story. The person living in Versailles to whom we had been directed as having related the tradition of the Queen's being at Trianon on October 5, 1789, was unable to remember anything at all about it.

The photographs of the Belvédère made it clear that it was not identical with the kiosk. On the many occasions on which Miss Jourdain went to the Trianon, she could never again find the places—not even the wood in which she had been. She assured me that the place was entirely different; the distances were much less than we had imagined; and the ground was so bare that the house and the Hameau were in full view of one another; and that there was nothing unnatural about the trees. Miss Jourdain brought back from Paris the books La Reine Marie Antoinette, by M. de Nolhac, and Le Petit Trianon, by Desjardins. We noted that M. de Nolhac related the traditional story of the

Queen's visit, and that the Comte de Vaudreuil, who betrayed the Queen by inciting her to the fatal acting of the Barbier de Séville in her own theater at Trianon, was a Creole and marked by smallpox.

Turning over the pages of Desjardins I found Wertmüller's portrait of the Queen, and exclaimed that it was the first of all the pictures I had seen which at all brought back the face of the lady that I had seen on my first visit.

In January 1904, Miss Jourdain went to the Comédie Française to see the Barbier de Séville, and noticed that the Alguazils standing round were dressed exactly like our garden officials, but had red stockings added. This was interesting, as the Comédie Française is the descendant of the royal private theater, and the old royal liveries worn by the subordinate actors (who were, in earlier times, the royal servants) are carefully reproduced at it.

Also, she reported that Almaviva was dressed in a dark cloak and a large Spanish hat, which was said to be the outdoor dress of French gentlemen of the period. On Monday, July 4, 1904, Miss Jourdain and I went to the Trianon, this being my second visit. We were accompanied by a friend who had not heard our story. On the Saturday of the same week (July 9) we went again unaccompanied.

Both days were brilliant and hot. On both occasions the dust, glare, trams, and comers and goers, contrasted with the quietness and solitude of our visit in 1901. We went up the lane as at the first time and turned to the right on reaching the building, which we had now learnt to call the logement du corps de gardes.

From this point everything was changed. The old wall facing us had gates, but they were closed, and the one through which we had seen the drive passing through a grove of trees seemed to have been closed for a very long time. We came directly to the gardener's house, which was quite different in appearance from the cottage described by Miss Jourdain in 1901, in front of which she saw the woman and the girl. Beyond the gardener's house was a parterre with flowerbeds, and a smooth lawn of many years' careful care. It did not seem to be the place where we had met the garden officials.

We spent a long time looking for the old paths. Not only was there no trace of them, but the distances were contracted, and all was on a smaller scale than I recollected. The kiosk was gone; so were the ravine and the little cascade which had fallen from a height above our heads, and the little bridge over the ravine was, of course, gone too. The large bridge with the Rocher over it, crossing one side of the lake at the foot of the Belvédère, had no resemblance to it. The trees were quite natural, and seemed to have been a good deal cleared out, making that part of the garden much less wooded and picturesque.

The English garden in front of the house was not shaded by many trees. We could see the house and the Hameau from almost every point. Instead of a much-shaded rough meadow continuing up to the wall of the terrace, there is now a broad gravel sweep beneath it, and the trees on the grass are gone.

Exactly where the lady was sitting we found a large spreading bush of, apparently, many years' growth. We did not recognize the present staircase, which leads up to the northwest end of the terrace, nor the extension of wall round which one has now to go in order to reach the staircase. We thought that we went up to the terrace from some point nearer to the house from the English garden: also, the present exit from the French garden to the avenue was not so near the house as we expected, nor was it so broad as we remembered it.

To add to the impossibility of recalling our first visit, in every corner we came across groups of noisy, merry people walking or sitting in the shade. Garden seats placed everywhere, and stalls for fruit and lemonade, took away from any idea of desolation. The commonplace, unhistorical atmosphere was totally inconsistent with the air of silent mystery by which we had been so much oppressed. Though for several years Miss Jourdain had assured me of the change, I had not expected such complete disillusionment.

One thing struck me greatly—people went wherever they liked, and no one would think of interfering to show the way, or to prevent anyone from going in any direction. We searched the place at our pleasure. We went to the Hameau, following the path taken by Miss Jourdain on January 2, 1902. We tried to find the thick wood in which she had lost her way, but there was nothing like it, and such paths as there are now being perfectly visible from one another, even in summer.

We asked a gardener sweeping one of the paths whether that part of the grounds had ever been a thick wood. He said he believed that it had been, but could give us no date beyond the fact that it was before his time—more than twenty years ago.

Looking For Evidence

On our return to Versailles we went into a bookseller's shop and asked if he had any maps or views of the Petit Trianon as it had been in old days. He showed us a picture (which he would not part with)

Time Travel – Fact Not Fiction

of the Jeu de Bague. We saw at once that the central building had some likeness to the kiosk, but the surrounding part was not like, and its position was unsuitable for our purpose.

We asked about the green uniforms of the garden officials, and he emphatically denied their existence. He said that "green was one of the colors of the royal liveries," and when we answered that three years before persons in long greenish coats had directed us in the grounds, he said it was "impossible, unless they were masqueraders."

One of the guards of the Palace also told us that "green was a royal livery and that now only the President had the right to use it on certain occasions." We asked how long the gardens had been thrown open to the public and people allowed to wander everywhere, and were told that it had been so for years, and this evidently implied a great many years.

The result of this expedition was to make us take a graver view of our first visit, and we resolved to look into the matter as carefully as we could, for no ordinary histories of the French Revolution supplied topographical details of the Queen's private garden. After some years, we have been able to collect many facts, small and unimportant in themselves, but together forming a single picture of strange significance to us.

This fascinating story has been the subject of controversy almost from the very beginning. Eleanor Jourdain and Anne Moberly had speculated that somehow they had passively viewed Marie Antoinette's thoughts. According to their hypothesis, the visions that had enveloped them were scenes from a vivid, melancholy daydream that once had filled the queen's mind.

Seeking to link their experience to Marie Antoinette's, they tracked down and studied documents from that period. A map drawn by the queen's architect suggested to them that a cottage had indeed stood where Miss Jourdain had seen one, although the site was now empty. They also discovered an architectural record from 1780 noting a small columned structure that they thought must be the kiosk they had seen.

Skeptics of the teachers' strange experiences have pointed out that poet Robert de Montesquiou and his friends often rehearsed historical plays near the Petit Trianon and the two women may have seen these amateur theatricals. However, this does little to explain the differences such as deep woods and buildings that no longer existed. The two teachers were convinced that they had encountered something unusual, perhaps a glimpse into the shadows of yesterday.

Time Travel – Fact Not Fiction

Many ghost sightings are readily explained as individuals who appear out of their normal location or time; but often the surroundings are also seen to change, giving the impression of a time slip. Are these glimpses into another time or does the witness actually travel through time by some currently unexplained method?

Chapter Four
People, Buildings and Towns From Beyond Time

The story of the two English schoolteachers and their amazing adventure in France is a good example of a type of haunting known as **retrocognition**, a term based on the Latin for backward knowing, percipients say they experience past events and environments as if transported back in time.

Rather than hauntings by spirits of the dead, perhaps these experiences are exactly what they seem to be, glimpses back in time. Perhaps even more amazing, these are situations where people have been physically transported back in time. Even though they are not often reported, these types of experiences may not be as rare as some may consider.

On October 3, 1963, Mrs. Coleen Buterbaugh, a secretary at Nebraska Wesleyan University, said that as she entered a room on campus she was struck by a strong odor and the realization of a penetrating silence as if she had been cut off from the world.

Glancing up, Buterbaugh saw a woman in an old-fashioned dress straining to reach the upper shelves of an old music cabinet. The figure had her back to Buterbaugh, who could tell that the woman was very tall and thin and that she wore her black hair in an old-fashioned bouffant style. Her clothes, including a long shirtwaisted dress, also appeared to be some thirty years out of date.

"She never moved," Buterbaugh reported. "It was as if I was looking at a photograph. She had her back to me, reaching up into one of the shelves of the cabinet with her right hand, and standing perfectly still. She was not transparent, she looked as solid and real as anyone else, and yet I knew she wasn't real. While I was looking at her, she just faded away."

When Buterbaugh looked out the window, she was taken aback when she saw that "there wasn't one modern thing out there. The street, which is less than a half block away from the building, was not even there and neither was the Willard House. That was when I realized that these people were not in my time, but that I was back in their time." As soon as the secretary stepped out of the room and into the hallway, she said, she reentered the present.

On May 10, 1973, Michigan's *Dearborn Press* carried a story about a young woman who stepped out of her time and into the past. Laura Jean Daniels was walking home from work one night when she noticed that her surroundings were suddenly no longer familiar.

"Even the pavement on the sidewalk was gone," Daniels said. "I was walking on a brick path."

The houses along the street had also disappeared, and several hundred feet ahead of her, at the end of the brick path, was a cottage she had never seen before.

Frightened, she continued along the path. As she neared the cottage, she saw a man and woman in old-fashioned clothes sitting in the garden. "They were embracing, and as I drew closer I could see the expression on the girl's face," Daniels told the reporter. "Believe me, she was in love."

Daniels was embarrassed to be witnessing so intimate a scene and she wondered how she could discreetly make her presence known, when a small dog came running up to her, barking madly. "The dog was quivering all over, like he was afraid," said Daniels.

"The man looked up and called to the dog and asked what the animal was barking at." At that point Daniels realized the man "couldn't see me, and yet I could smell the flowers and feel the gate beneath my hand. Plus the dog could obviously see me, as he was looking right at me as he barked."

Confused, she turned and looked behind her—and saw familiar surroundings. "There was my street," she related. "But I could still feel the gate in my hand."

However, when she turned back to look toward the cottage again, it was not there. Instead, she said, "I was standing right in the middle of my own block, just a few doors from home." She never saw the cottage or the couple again. It was as if Laura Jean Daniels had briefly walked through a hole from her time to another and then out again.

Buildings and People From Time And Space

When I was a young man, a friend of mine owned a beat-up old car that we would occasionally use to take rides out into the countryside. The town where I grew up was surrounded by mile after mile of

Time Travel – Fact Not Fiction

farmland, so it was easy to discover roads you had never encountered before. Early one evening and miles from home, we had a flat tire. We were in the middle of nowhere. There was nothing but cornfields as far as the eye could see. Fortunately, my friend had a spare, but the jack was old and not very sturdy and we struggled to change the stubborn tire.

Suddenly, an old man appeared out of nowhere and offered to lend us a hand. Startled by his sudden appearance I asked our Good Samaritan "Where did you come from?"

"Why from my house right there," he pointed to a small white house a few hundred feet off the road. This surprised me because I was sure that we were miles from any house when we pulled over. The man quickly got the jack fixed and soon the spare tire was on and we were on our way.

As we drove off, I looked back and I could see the old man slowly making his way back down the walk to his house. I also noticed that alongside the walk on each side were neatly trimmed and beautiful rose bushes, what we used to call wild rose bushes.

I would have soon forgotten about this incident if it hadn't been for my mothers insistence a few days later that we repay the old man for his help.

"He probably lives all alone way out there," my mother said. "It isn't right that we don't send him something to thank him for his kindness."

She handed me a freshly baked pie with the instructions to take it immediately to our kind benefactor.

My friend and I were familiar enough with the area that we soon found our way back onto the road that ran in front of the old man's house. However, when we arrived, we were startled to find that instead of a small white house, there was instead a pile of broken timbers and the remains of an old foundation to show where a house once stood.

"This can't be the right place," my friend said.

I started to agree when I noticed that the walkway leading up to the house was enclosed by wild rose bushes. Now, instead of neatly trimmed plants, the bushes were tall and wild. They obviously had not been taken care of for a long time.

We got out of the car to see if we could ascertain our location. Even though it looked the same, we were certain that this couldn't be the place where we had our trouble a few days before. As we stood looking around, I noticed at the side of the road the remnants of the blown tire we had recently changed.

"This must be the place," I said to my friend pointing out the old tire.

"It can't be," my friend said quietly. "It's all gone. There's nothing here, nothing."

As we stood there alongside the lonely country road, we realized that we were at the right location, but the house and the old man had long since gone. Had we seen a ghost, or did the old man somehow jump forward in time to lend a hand to a couple of teenagers?

Either way, the realization that something extremely unusual had happened prompted us to quickly get back into the car and leave the area. Until the day he passed away, my friend refused to discuss the incident with me and I often wonder just what exactly happened to us on that quiet country road.

Like my own strange experience off the back roads of Time and Space, other people over the years may have taken a wrong turn somewhere and ended up face to face with the unknown. Once again, we see evidence, albeit anecdotal, that there are hidden forces that occasionally rip open holes in time. These time slips are a purely natural phenomenon that may demonstrate a science beyond our current knowledge of physics, but still a natural event all the same.

What Did The Roman Girl See?

One of the strangest reports of a time slip came from a village near Lake Neuchatel in Switzerland in the early 1960s. A British tourist—identified in accounts of the case as Mr. B—was with two American companions, Charles Muses, a researcher and writer on parapsychological subjects, and Muse's wife.

The three were visiting the ruins of an old Roman theater where they found that much of the stone stage remained, as well as some of the tiers of seats that rose up the sides of the theater with high walls behind them.

Mounting the stage, Mr. B decided to test the theater's acoustics by standing center stage and speaking in a normal voice. His friends called back from the top row of seats that they could hear him perfectly. Then he stepped down into the orchestra pit. Suddenly, he said, he seemed to slip centuries into the past. According to his story, the crumbled sides of the theater became whole, and missing rows of seats appeared as if from thin air.

Time Travel – Fact Not Fiction

As he stood in shock, a large crowd of people in Roman dress poured in and began filling the seats. Scanning the unfamiliar scene, he noticed a very pretty girl dressed in yellow in one of the upper rows.

As he watched, she stared straight at him and then plucked at the clothing of her companions and pointed him out with her finger, apparently shocked by his appearance. Her friends seemed unable to see him.

A moment later a young man walked on stage and began playing a lute of ancient form. Mr. B said he heard only the first notes; almost at once the scene began to fade away. As it did, the vision of the Roman theater and the girl in yellow vanished, and he found himself once again in the present.

He later said he had found the experience "strange," but also enjoyable, and regretted that it had ended so quickly. Relating the experience to a writer, he exclaimed, "How strange I must have looked to a Roman girl."

A Visit To The Evelyn Family Church

This case was originally reported to the Society for Psychical Research in London in 1956. However, it wasn't until 1973 that the couple who shared the adventure openly related their story to psychical researcher Mary Rose Barrington.

During the summer of 1954, Mr. and Mrs. George Benson (pseudonym) were preoccupied with an exhibition that was taking up most of their time. They had been married for five years and were antique dealers. Being overworked and generally worn out, they decided to give themselves a day off and spend a whole Sunday walking in the Surrey Hills.

But when they got up early on the scheduled morning, Mrs. Benson was afflicted by a feeling of black depression. Not wanting to spoil the day's outing, she said nothing to her husband about how she felt. The Bensons intended to spend some time at the Evelyn family church at Wotton. The church lies at the end of a minor road on the north side of the main road from Dorking.

The couple ended up spending more time at the church and in the churchyard than they had originally intended, most of the time inspecting tombs and reading their inscriptions. They noted that this was the first time they had ever found the gates to the tomb inside the church open.

Time Travel – Fact Not Fiction

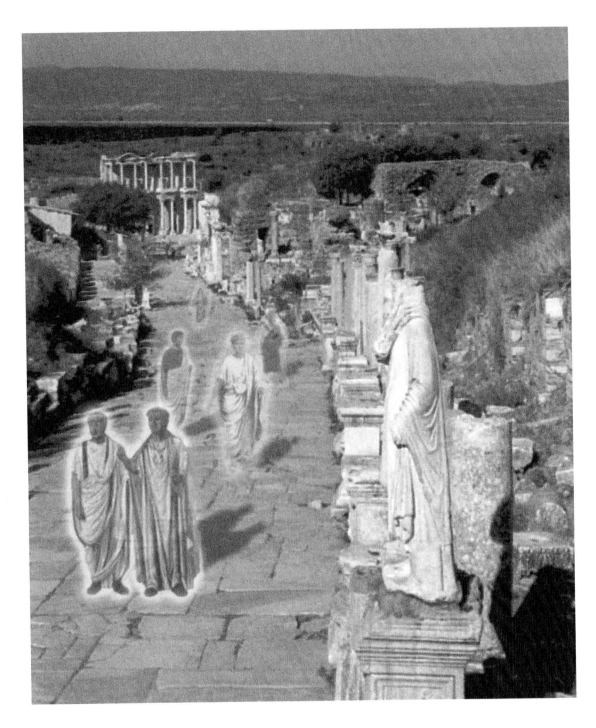

The ruins of the old Roman theater seemed to slip centuries into the past.
The crumbled sides of the theater became whole and missing rows of seats
appeared from thin air. A large crowd of people in Roman dress poured
in and began filling the seats as a young man walked on stage and began
playing a lute of ancient form.

Time Travel – Fact Not Fiction

When they came out of the churchyard gate sometime later, they turned right and found themselves facing an overgrown path, bordered by high bushes on either side. Following the path, they climbed for a considerable time and finally came to a wide clearing where there was a wooden bench. This seemed like a perfect place to survey their surroundings so the couple sat down.

To the left of the bench was an expanse of grass, with woodlands lying about 25 yards away behind it. To the right was a steep falling-away of the land. Mrs. Benson later said she felt sure about the height of the location because the view was consistent with a view from a hill and "down in the valley below." She could hear what sounded like wood being chopped as well as the barking of a dog. She felt uneasy but she didn't know why.

As he sat on the bench, Mr. Benson glanced at his watch and observed with surprise that it was already noon. Suddenly all became silent and the birds seemed to stop singing. Mrs. Benson started to feel cold and was overwhelmed with fear. Then she saw three figures standing in the clearing.

The three figures were wearing black clerical garb. The man in the middle had a round, friendly face but the other two radiated hatred and hostility. Mrs. Benson felt sure that these three men somehow belonged in the past.

Mrs. Benson told her husband that she wanted to leave. Mr. Benson, aware that his wife had undergone some sort of unpleasant experience, was more than willing to move on. They walked a little farther and began to descend from the rise. Soon they were on one of the paths that cross a local railway line and they walked over it. Strangely, they then laid down and went to sleep. To this day they do not remember leaving the area and cannot say whether they walked back to Dorking or returned to the road to take the bus. All they recall is that they arrived back at Dorking some hours later and took the train home to Battersea.

Over the next two years, Mrs. Benson never entirely recovered from the fear she had felt when she saw the three figures in the clearing. The experience practically obsessed her and she came to believe there was something about the experience she had to face and overcome. So almost exactly two years later, Mrs. Benson set out by herself for Wotton with the intention of revisiting the church.

By the time she arrived at the churchyard she already sensed that things were different. She headed for the church, looked around inside, wandered around the tombstones and returned to the gate, naturally expecting to come to the path leading to the hillside. But there was no path. There was nothing even remotely resembling the hillside that she and her husband remembered climbing.

She was so taken aback that she sought out a local resident who claimed that he knew the area well and that he couldn't think of anywhere that looked like the scene she described to him. Nor did the man know of any wooden bench. He insisted that such a landscape was not to be found anywhere near the church.

Mrs. Benson returned home and told her husband about her remarkable visit. Unable to believe her, he vowed to investigate the situation himself. The next Sunday he visited the church arriving at around noon as the congregation was beginning to leave. He approached someone who turned out to be a woodsman on the Wotton estate.

Mr. Benson described the area (the vanished landscape) he had seen during his previous visit and asked the man if he could think of any local site that fit the description. The woodsman said he couldn't and went on to state categorically that there were no wooden seats or benches on the Wotton estate and that, so far as he knew, there never had been.

Later investigation by Mary Rose Barrington determined that the round-faced man seen by Mrs. Benson could have been a character called "Soapy Sam," more properly known as Bishop Wilberforce who died in the 17th - Century under mysterious circumstances in the nearby woods. Barrington speculates that the Bensons deviated from their perception of "consensus" reality and were able to bend reality temporarily into a new shape and visit a time long since passed away.

The Restaurant At The Edge Of Time

One of the strangest stories to come out of the state of Wyoming occurred in March 1959. Bob Wetzel (pseudonym) was stationed at Lowry Air Force Base in Denver, Colorado. He and two friends were driving up to visit Bob's wife Sharon, who was living in Worland.

As the three men were leaving the Cheyenne city limits, a blinding spring snowstorm hit. It normally took only a half hour to get from Cheyenne to Chugwater. However, this trip through the blizzard took an hour and a half. By now the roads were ice-covered and the conditions continued to worsen.

The travelers were relieved when they unexpectedly came across a restaurant almost hidden in the blowing snow.

Time Travel – Fact Not Fiction

Bob later told writer Debra Munn that they were so glad to find a place to come in out of the storm and have dinner. They pulled off to the left side of the road and walked across the street and into the building through swinging doors in the front. The restaurant was empty except for the three men and the staff. Two young women dressed in long white dresses with black and white aprons waited on the travelers, who, after their long drive through the snow were famished and quickly ordered steaks.

When they finished their meal, they were surprised to see the tab on the bill. It came to only nine dollars for the three meals. They were so pleased that they left five one-dollar bills as a tip.

"You should have seen how surprised the waitresses were," said Bob. "They thanked me, walked us to the door, and told us to be careful, since it was still snowing so hard you could barely see."

The three men were soon back on the road again and made it to Worland with no difficulties. When they got there, they told Bob's wife Sharon and her parents about the nice restaurant they had found. They decided to stop there again on their way back. When Sharon made the return trip with her husband, the weather was clear and they had no trouble getting to Chugwater.

This was before the highways were put in and you had to drive right through the middle of the town. Bob remembered that as they had come down the hill from Denver heading north, the restaurant had been the third or fourth business on the left-hand side of the street.

"But this time it just wasn't there." Bob said. "There wasn't even any building on the site. We were looking at a vacant lot."

Unable to believe their eyes, Bob and one of his friends walked to a nearby hamburger stand, where Bob spoke to an elderly gentleman.

"I think his name was Charlie, and I told him that we had come through Chugwater and eaten at a restaurant that was no longer there," Bob recalled. The man looked confused but then realized what Charlie was talking about.

"Son, the place that you describe burned down years and years ago, and this has been a vacant lot since then," the old man answered.

"There's no way," Bob said. "We were just in there," and he began to describe the two waitresses who had served them.

"Son," the man said again. "That place burned down and the two women you described perished in the fire, but that was a long time ago."

Time Travel – Fact Not Fiction

Looking back on the experience, Bob could recall nothing unusual about the restaurant itself, except for the low cost of the meal. The food and drink seemed real, as did the two waitresses. There was nothing "ghost-like" about the situation at all. However, Bob did remember thinking at the time that the complexions of both waitresses were very white, and later he realized that their long dresses and aprons might have belonged to an earlier time.

Was this a haunting? All three men were certain that what they had experienced was real and had nothing to do with ghosts or spirits. However, they could not explain the fact that they ate at a restaurant that no longer existed in their time. An event that is not as rare as is often assumed.

Preview Of An Air Raid

J. Bernard Hutton in his book *On The Other Side of Reality*, relates two amazing stories about apparent time slips. The first is a personal account by Hutton who was a German newspaper reporter in 1932. Hutton and photographer Joachim Brandt were sent to do a story on the Hamburg-Altona shipyards.

An executive showed them around the place and by the end of the afternoon their assignment was finished. Just as they left the yards, the two men heard the drone of aircraft overhead, and in a short while the noise of antiaircraft guns drowned out all other sounds.

Darkness had fallen and soon the two men saw bombs exploding all around them. Before long, the place was an inferno, and what they had at first taken for a practice drill was all too clearly a full-scale air raid.

They turned back to ask the guard at the gate if they could do anything to help. They were threateningly told to go about their business, and so Hutton and his photographer drove back to Hamburg, positive that they had witnessed an incredible event.

Although the sky had been dark throughout the attack, they were surprised to find Hamburg going about its everyday business by the light of an ordinary late afternoon. They stopped their car and looked back toward the shipyards. They were intact and unharmed in the fading daylight.

When Brandt's photographs were developed, he had kept on shooting throughout the air raid, they showed nothing unusual, and when the editor heard their story he accused them of being drunk on the job.

Time Travel – Fact Not Fiction

Just before World War II broke out, Hutton left Germany to live in England. There, in 1943, he saw a newspaper account of a highly successful night raid by the Royal Air Force on the Hamburg shipyards. He sought more details of the attack and confirmed what he had guessed: the scene of destruction that he and Brandt had witnessed in the spring of 1932 had been real after all; they had seen it 11 years before it happened.

Flight Into The Future

In 1934, Victor Goddard of the Royal Air Force was lost. Somewhere over Scotland a heavy storm had caught him, and now he needed to find a landmark. He eased his Hawker Hart biplane down through the clouds, hoping to find clear weather below him and perhaps to catch a glimpse of Drem, an abandoned airfield that he thought was somewhere in the vicinity.

His instincts were good. Drem was not far ahead of him, and from it he could take new bearings. Then, when he was about a quarter of a mile from the airfield, something unusual happened. "Suddenly," he wrote later, "the area was bathed in an ethereal light as though the sun were shining on a midsummer day."

Goddard could see below him that Drem was far from deserted. It was a hive of activity, of mechanics in blue overalls at work on yellow planes, all bright in the sunlight. He flew over them at an altitude of no more than 50 feet and everything seemed to be completely normal. Although he was a little surprised that no one looked up as his plane went over and headed back into the low clouds. Now confident of his directions, Goddard continued his flight with no further problems.

Several days later Goddard inquired about the status of Drem and was shocked to learn that the airfield was indeed abandoned and had been for almost ten years.

In 1938, with the threat of war growing daily, Drem was reopened as an air force flying school, and the color of British training planes changed from silver to yellow. Goddard remarked when visiting the airfield in 1940 that this was exactly what he had seen while flying overhead in 1934. He was at a loss to explain, however, how he had managed to see an airfield that would not become active until four years later.

This story may sound familiar to students of Fortean phenomenon, as it has been retold in several different ways and different locations.

Time Travel – Fact Not Fiction

A recent incarnation of this story allegedly involved a pilot named Frederick Howard who in 1956 spotted an airport in Duquesne, Indiana with a field full of airplanes, all of 1920 and 30-vintage. The airport itself supposedly appeared as it looked in 1934. However, this story is a hoax as research has failed to uncover any town in Indiana called Duquesne.

Bold Street Time Slip

Time is thought to be unstoppable in its relentless push towards the future. Humans perceive themselves as bound up in time as an insect in amber. Forever imprisoned and forced to reconcile with the regularity and inevitability of change. The past is gone – the present, fleeting – and the future is unknown. Or is it?

If a Merseyside policeman by the name of Frank was asked, he may have an entirely different opinion on the subject of time.

On a sunny Saturday afternoon in July of 1996, Frank and his wife, Carol was visiting Liverpool's Bold Street area for some shopping. At Central Station, the pair split up; Carol went to Dillons Bookshop and Frank went to HMV to look for a CD he wanted. As he walked up the incline near the Lyceum Post Office/Café building that lead onto Bold Street, Frank suddenly noticed he had entered a strange "oasis of quietness."

Suddenly, a small box van that looked like something out of the 1950s sped across his path, honking its horn as it narrowly missed him. Frank noticed the name on the van's side: "Caplan's." When he looked down, the confused policeman saw that he was unexpectedly standing in the road. The off-duty policeman crossed the road and saw that Dillons Book Store now had "Cripps" over its entrances. More confused, he looked in to see not books, but women's handbags and shoes.

Looking around, Frank realized people were dressed in clothes that appeared to be from the 1940s. Suddenly, he spotted a young girl in her early 20's dressed in a lime-colored sleeveless top. The handbag she was carrying had a popular brand name on it, which reassured the policeman that maybe he was still partly in 1996. It was a paradox, but he was relieved, and he followed the girl into Cripps.

As the pair went inside, Frank watched in amazement as the interior of the building completely changed in a flash to that of Dillons Bookshop of 1996.

The girl turned to leave and Frank lightly grasped the girl's arm to attract attention and said, "Did you see that?"

Time Travel – Fact Not Fiction

She replied, "Yeah! I thought it was a clothes shop. I was going to look around, but it's a bookshop."

It was later determined that Cripps and Caplan's were businesses based in Liverpool during the 1950s. Whether these businesses were based in the locations specified in the story has not been confirmed.

Time Slips or Hauntings?

In 1997 "Lyn" lived in a small Australian outback town that was built in 1947 and had changed little since that time.

"I was driving toward the main intersection of the town, when suddenly I felt a change in the air. It wasn't the classic colder feeling, but a change, like a shift in atmosphere. The air felt denser somehow. As I slowed at the intersection, I seemed to be suddenly transported back in time to approximately 1950. The road was dirt, the trees were gone and coming toward me to cross the intersection was an old black car, something like a Vanguard or old FJ Holden. As the car passed through the intersection the driver was looking back at me in total astonishment before he accelerated. From what I could see he was dressed in similar 1950s fashion, complete with hat.

"This whole episode lasted perhaps 20 seconds and was repeated at least five times during my time there, always at the exact spot. I tried to make out the registration plate number but the car was covered in dust."

Lyn wondered if there is someone out there still living who remembers seeing a strange sight at the intersection back in the 50s...of a weird car with a bug-eyed woman at the wheel.

Derek E. tells another interesting time slip story. When he was a child, his father was a taxi driver in Glasgow, Scotland. One day in the late 1960s, Derek's father was driving in the north of the city along Maryhill Road near Queen's Cross, one of the older parts of town and once its own separate community outside the city.

"One minute it was now," Derek wrote, "cars, buses, modern clothes, tarmac roads etc. – and the next thing my dad knew he was in some earlier time. It was certainly pre-Victorian given the clothes he described people wearing, horses, rough road, lower buildings, people in rough clothes and bonnets etc. It lasted as long as it took him to be aware of it and then it vanished and he was back in the here & now."

Derek also reported that in the 1980's, he and his wife were on a driving holiday in the North York Moors in England. They went to a

Time Travel – Fact Not Fiction

tiny coastal village called Staithes, which had a steep winding and narrowing road down to the harbor, with the entrance to the houses and narrow footway at a higher level of three or four feet.

"We parked at the top of the village, hamlet really, where the tourist buses and cars had to stop and made our way down on foot. What I remember is a brilliantly sunny day with lots of other people around, but as we made our way down, it just suddenly seemed as if no one else were there but my wife and me. An old woman appeared on the footway opposite us. It became cooler and duller. She asked, in what seemed to me an old-fashioned and very polite way, what year it was. Now lots of old people get confused and it could have been that, but what I remember vividly is her black clothes – handmade, rough and with hand-sewn buttons – really big compared with modern ones. Her shoes were very old fashioned with much higher and chunkier heels than you'd see an older person wearing nowadays. In the time it took me to turn to my wife and say, 'Did you see that?' she was gone. The sun was back and so were all the people. My wife had also seen the same old woman and felt the same chill."

Derek's experience seems strikingly similar to traditional ghost stories. Many ghost sightings are readily explained as individuals who appear out of their normal location or time; but often the ghost also seems to change the surroundings of the witness, giving the impression of a time slip. What is open to question is whether these are glimpses into another time or does the witness or the ghost actually travel in time? Perhaps it is simply different sides of the same coin.

The Hotel From Nowhere

In 1984 Yorkshire Television, filming the series Arthur C. Clarke's *World of Strange Powers*, recreated the amazing story of two couples from Dover, England who apparently spent the night in a hotel from the past.

Their story started in October 1979 when Len and Cynthia Gisby and their friend's Geoff and Pauline Simpson, all decided to take a trip into France. Their plan was to take the ferry across the English Channel and drive through France to northern Spain for two weeks.

On October 3, around 9:30 PM, they were on the autoroute north of Montelimar, France, far to the south. It had been a pleasant day but they were tired and the encroaching darkness led them to look for a place to stay. They came across a nice motel and decided to stop there for the night. When Len went inside, he spoke with a man in the

Time Travel – Fact Not Fiction

lobby who was dressed in a rather strange plum-colored uniform. The man informed Len that there was no room at the motel.

"However," Len was told, "if you take the road off the autoroute there, you will find a small hotel. They will have rooms."

Len thanked the man and the party drove away. As they drove on Cynthia and Pauline commented on the old buildings lining the roadside. The posters plastered on them were promoting a circus. "It was a very old-fashioned circus," Pauline remarked. "That's why we took so much interest."

The men were more interested in the road itself, cobbled and very narrow. When no other traffic passed by, they began to doubt the wisdom of this plan. Cynthia noticed some lights ahead and they pulled to a stop in front of a building by the roadside. It was long and low, with a row of brightly lit windows. There were some men standing in front of it.

Cynthia got out but came back to the car. "It's not a hotel. It's an inn." So they drove on, past a long border of trees which now lined the road.

They soon reached two other buildings. One appeared to be a police station. The other had a sign that read "Hotel." Thankful that their journey was over, Len got out and went to ask for accommodations. He came back sighing with relief. "They have rooms." And so the tired travelers unloaded their bags.

The hotel was an unusual ranch-style building. It had just two stories and looked quaint and old-fashioned. Because none of the four spoke French and the hotel manager apparently spoke no English, they made themselves known as best they could and were shown to their rooms.

On their way they noticed that the building's interior were as strange as its exterior. Everything was old and made of heavy wood. There were no tablecloths on the tables in the dining room and there seemed to be no telephones or other modern conveniences anywhere in the building. Upstairs in their rooms the beds were large but had no pillows, only bolsters. The sheets were heavy and the mattresses sagged in the middle. The doors had no locks, just wooden catches. The two couples had to share a bathroom with old-fashioned plumbing and soap attached to a metal bar stuck in the wall. Tired from their long day, everyone went straight to bed and slept soundly through the night. The next morning they went down to the dining room for breakfast. The meal was simple, consisting of bread, jam and coffee. "The coffee tasted black and horrible," Geoff recalled with disgust.

Time Travel – Fact Not Fiction

While they were eating, a woman came into the room and sat down opposite them. She wore a silk evening gown and carried a dog under her arm. "It was strange," remembered Pauline. "It looked like she had just come in from a ball but it was seven in the morning. I couldn't take my eyes off of her."

Then two gendarmes arrived, wearing deep blue uniforms and capes and large, peaked hats. "They were nothing like the gendarmes we saw anywhere else in France," Geoff said. "Their uniforms seemed to be very old." Len and Geoff decided to ask the gendarmes the best way to take the autoroute to Avignon and the Spanish border. However, the policemen shrugged at the word "autoroute" and plainly did not know the term. Geoff presumed that Len's attempts at French were just not successful.

Before they left, it was decided to take some pictures of the quaint surroundings, so Geoff took his camera out and photographed Pauline standing by the shuttered windows. Len took several photographs of Cynthia inside the hotel silhouetted against the window.

With the car packed and all three ready to leave, Len went across to the manager and asked for the bill. The man scribbled a sum on a piece of paper and presented the bill which amounted to the astonishing price of just 19 francs (about $3.00). Even though the couples tried to tell the manager that the price seemed too low for the four of them, he indicated that the price was indeed correct. Since there was no sense in arguing, the couples paid up in cash and promptly left.

The remainder of their two-week trip in Spain was uneventful and on the way back they decided to stop at the same hotel. After all, not many places offer such unique services at such low prices.

The weather was bad but they found the turnoff easily and drove down it. "There are the circus signs," Pauline noted. "This is definitely the right road."

But they could not find the hotel. They were concerned enough to return to the motel on the autoroute and ask directions. Not only did the man there know of no such hotel but he denied any knowledge of the man in the plum-colored uniform who had directed them to it in the first place. Three times they drove up and down the road. But there was no hotel. It had vanished into thin air. The area looked somehow different as well, although no one could explain why. Utterly bewildered, they continued into Lyon where they spent the night in a local bed-and-breakfast. The bill for the four amounted to 247 francs (about $40).

Time Travel – Fact Not Fiction

At the end of their vacation the mystery of the vanishing hotel deepened when they got back their holiday photographs. Geoff had taken 20 photos and Len had 36. The three photographs of the hotel, one by Geoff and two by Len, had all been taken in the middle of the respective films. But none of the hotel shots were returned. In fact, there were no spoiled negatives. Each film had its full quota of photographs. It was as if the pictures that they had taken did not exist. They had disappeared just like the hotel.

During the filming of Arthur C. Clarke's *World of Strange Powers*, the Simpsons and the Gisbys were flown back to the area and were filmed reconstructing attempts to find the hotel.

"We did some looking around on our own while we were there," said Geoff Simpson. "We even thought we had found the place. But it was not our hotel, just an old house, nothing like the hotel. At the place where we were all sure the hotel had been there was nothing at all."

The French tourist board in Lyon says that there is no hotel like the one the Gisbys and Simpsons describe.

In July 1985, paranormal researcher Jenny Randles spent an evening with the Simpsons, in the company of fellow researchers Linda Taylor and Harry Harris. Harris had arranged for the couple to be interviewed and hypnotically regressed by psychiatrist Dr. Albert Keller at his Manchester surgery.

Pauline could not be hypnotized but Geoff Simpson proved an excellent subject, reliving the events with emotion and awe. A detailed description of the adventure was offered but no new elements were uncovered.

"You tell us what the answer is. We only know what happened," Geoff concludes.

Was this an example of a time slip? Did four people somehow leave their time and enter the past? If this is the case then some questions must be asked. How is it that the people around the strange hotel did not notice the car the travelers drove up in. If this was a case of time travel you would think that a futuristic car would have garnered some attention. Also, why did the hotel manager not notice that the cash paid to him was 1979 currency? You would think that this would have appeared odd to anyone living that far back in the past. This story could show that some time slips could be journeys to parallel dimensions that are superficially similar to our world. There are no reasonable explanations, only the enduring mystery of four people who spent the night in a hotel that simple was not there.

Time Travel – Fact Not Fiction

Martin Jeffrey, co-editor with Louise Jeffrey of the website www.mysterymag.com, speculates that time slips can be recreated or induced using a "trigger factor," which "...occurs when one is interested in his surroundings but is not concentrating on them; a slip occurs at a precise place and moment and the witness is thrust seemingly into another time."

Jeffrey cites the case of Alice Pollock, who at Leeds Castle in Kent "experienced what could be called a classic time slip. Alice was experimenting in Henry VIII's rooms by touching objects in an attempt to experience events from another time. After a period of receiving no impressions whatsoever, the room suddenly changed. It lost its modern, comfortable appearance to become cold and bare. The carpet had disappeared and there were now logs burning on the fire. A tall woman in a white dress was walking up and down the room; her face seemed to be in deep concentration. Not long after, the room returned to its original state.

Later research found that the rooms had been the prison of Queen Joan of Navarre, Henry V's stepmother, who had been accused of witchcraft by her husband.

It could be that the witness triggers time slips, whether they blank their mind at a precise moment and the slip occurs, or the witness touches something that holds the memory of a previous time.

"The simplest explanation is probably the psychometric hypothesis," noted Colin Wilson and John Grant in **The Directory of Possibilities**. "In the mid-nineteenth century, Dr. Joseph Rodes Buchanan of the Covington Medical Institute performed experiments that convinced him that certain of his students could hold letters in their hands and accurately describe the character of the writer. He became convinced that all objects carry their history photographed in them. Buchanan wrote: 'The past is entombed in the present. The discoveries of psychometry will enable us to explore the history of Man as those of geology enable us to explore the history of Earth.' Clearly, psychometry may be seen as a form of time slip."

Hans Holzer, better known for his books about ghosts and hauntings, investigated the strange story of Robert Cory who came across a town where none should have been.

In 1964, Cory took a vacation trip by car to visit his future in-laws at Kenwick, Washington. His fiancé was with him, but he left her with her parents after a few days to drive back to Burbank by himself.

The fall weather was dry and pleasant when he left the state of Washington. It would be a 12-hour trip down to the Los Angeles area.

Time Travel – Fact Not Fiction

Cory left Washington around 11:30 PM and when he crossed the Oregon state line it was already dark. The weather conditions were good, the sky was clear and there was nothing to hinder Cory on his trip. He soon started to climb into the mountains on a long, winding, road going south.

About four hours after he had left Washington, around 3:30 AM, he was rounding a bend and suddenly he found himself in a snowstorm. One moment it was a clear, dry autumn night—the next, a raging snowstorm.

"I slowed down. I was scared," he explained. "The road was narrow, mountains on one side, a drop on the other."

Cory could not drive any further through the mysterious storm, when he noticed a bright light a little way down the road. When he got to the light, it turned out to be a road sign, reflecting light from somewhere.

He was now on top of a hill, so he coasted downhill until the car came to a full stop. Cory looked out and discovered that he had rolled into some sort of village for he saw houses. When he got out of the car, he found himself on a bumpy street.

The town looked like something from the old west, with a bumpy, dirt road and wooden sidewalks. One building had the word "hotel" on it, and he walked to it and knocked at the door. Everything was dark, but the door was open and he entered the lobby of the hotel. He called out into the darkness, but no one appeared to be around, the lobby was completely empty. However, there was a potbellied stove with a fire in it.

Cory moved near the stove to get warm. To one side he noticed a barbershop chair. In the back he saw a desk and a big clock. There were animal heads hung on the walls and a calender dating back to the early 1900s.

Also, some notices on a board on the wall with dates in the late 1800s. To his left he saw a phone booth. It turned out this was an antique with a crank to operate. The telephone had a sign reading "Crank Box For Operator." Unfortunately the phone did not seem to be working so he settled himself down on a sofa to wait out the night.

The warmth of the stove soon lulled Cory to sleep, but he was awakened by a noise and he saw on old man wearing big boots and old overalls coming down the stairs.

"He sat down in a rocking chair across from the stove. He saw me and we nodded at each other. Finally he said to me, 'You couldn't fall asleep . . . why don't you fall asleep?' I said to him, 'Well, that's all right I'm not really sleepy." But he replied, 'No, you couldn't fall asleep, it's okay, it's okay.'"

Cory fell back to sleep, but he woke up several times during the night to see the man still slowly rocking in his chair by the fire. He slept until daybreak and when he woke up and opened his eyes, he saw eight or ten men walking around, talking, doing different things.

"I sat up but no one paid attention to me, as if I were not there. But I got up and said hello to one of them, and he said hello back to me. There were a couple men hanging around the stove with their backs to me, talking, and then there was a man standing behind the barber chair shaving somebody who wasn't even there."

According to Cory the people in the hotel seemed like normal people except he had the feeling they were in some way smaller. They all looked very old like the first man he saw coming down the stairs.

"One of the men was walking back and forth in the lobby talking to nobody, arguing, carrying on a conversation all by himself. I turned to the three men around the stove and asked, 'Is there a gas station around?' Now I could understand they were speaking to me but the words made no sense."

Suddenly from the back of the room a voice called out "Breakfast. Come, breakfast." The old man that Cory had seen the night before came over and grabbed his arm and said, "Come have breakfast." However, Cory had become frightened by his strange surroundings and backed off away from the man. At that point everyone in the room turned around and then started walking toward him, slowly, normally.

Cory asked, "Where am I. Where am I?" The old man said to him, "Don't worry. Don't worry." But Cory had become extremely frightened by the strangeness of the situation and he quickly turned and walked out of the building and got into his car.

"I drove down this bumpy road and I saw the faces of the men looking out of the windows of the hotel behind me. I could clearly see tears rolling down the face of the old man as I drove away. I also saw people on the street. One of them a woman, she wore a long dress like the Salvation Army women do."

As Cory drove past the people on the sidewalk, something like a cloud or fog suddenly appeared and he was enveloped in it for about 30 seconds.

Time Travel – Fact Not Fiction

"The next thing I know I came out into one of the brightest, shiniest days you could imagine. I drove another half a mile or so until I saw a gas station. I was back in today's life."

Later, when Cory and his fiancé tried to retrace his steps, they found no town or buildings where he had said he stopped for the night. People who lived nearby told them that a small village had at one time been at that location, but it had been abandoned years ago and the buildings torn down. Hans Holzer wondered if the combined energies of the people Cory encountered were strong enough, and their fear of leaving their little world powerful enough, to create a little enclave in Time and Space, forever keeping them from going on with the rest of the world.

They existed in a past reality that remained in a constant state of "Now." Never changing, always the same, until some unfortunate traveler, lost in the night, inadvertently enters their existence. Possibly all of the stories in this chapter deal with the same phenomenon—people and places trapped in a frozen moment in time.

What conclusions can be made from these anecdotal tales? Did these people actually travel, albeit briefly, into the past to glimpse scenes that once were? Or were they caught up in a form of haunting where, like an old movie, they saw a scene that had somehow been implanted in a location and allowed to "play back" again for those sensitive enough to pick up the lingering impressions?

However, if time slips are a form of haunting, what explanation can be offered to the experience of a Mr. Squirrel, who in 1973 went into a stationer's shop in Great Yarmouth to buy some envelopes. He was served by a woman in Edwardian dress and bought three dozen envelopes for a shilling. He noticed that the building was extremely silent – there was no traffic noise. On visiting the shop three weeks later, he found it completely changed and modernized; the assistant, an elderly lady, denied that there had been any other assistant in the shop the previous week. Even though the envelopes disintegrated quickly, Mr. Squirrel was able to track down the manufacturers, who said that such envelopes had ceased to be manufactured fifteen years before. How can a haunting produce such physical evidence?

Time slips are "often accompanied by feelings of depression, eeriness and a marked sense of silence, deeper than normally experienced," posits author Andrew MacKenzie in his book *Adventures in Time: Encounters With the Past*, drawing this conclusion based on the Versailles time slip accounts as well as his own interviews with people who have experienced the phenomenon. "It is interesting to note that on August 10, 1901, the day of Annie Moberly and Eleanor

Time Travel – Fact Not Fiction

Jourdain's experience, electrical storms were recorded over Europe and the atmosphere was heavy with electricity. Could this have led to an alteration in the local temporal field around Versailles?"

Perhaps there is a natural phenomenon that under the right conditions and location can produce briefly a doorway to another time and place. Even though this may sound outrageous, this natural "time machine" could show that modern concepts and perceptions of time need to be seriously reconsidered.

Could it be possible that the past and future may be closer to us then thought with current scientific theories? With the right frame of mind and the right natural conditions, the barriers of Time and Space that have traditionally kept mankind locked into place may finally be broken, allowing the mysteries of the world and the universe to be finally revealed.

Chapter Five
Strange Talents

The flow of time is considered to be ever-constant, unyieldingly flowing from the present into the future. Yet how accurate is this belief? We have seen testimony from individuals who have experienced what can only be described as visits into the past or future. If these incidents happened as described, then our current theories about the physics of Time and Space are wrong, or at least woefully inadequate.

Time as a dimension is probably extremely yielding to natural and conscious energies. Natural events such as electrical storms and the Earth's magnetic field seem at times to be able to break down the barriers that separate the past, present and future. Since these natural energies are constantly flooding our environment, then it could be presumed that time is forever swirling around, mixing past, present and future together with just the thinnest wall of energy acting as a barrier.

The energy that separates time is in constant flux, with holes appearing and disappearing in fractions of seconds. This flux can be manipulated by all kinds of different energies, this includes conscious energies, the power of the human mind.

While most slips in Time and Space are random events, some occur because of the influence of a conscious mind. Sometimes this influence is an unconscious desire made reality, much to the chagrin of the individual who's hidden yearnings manifest as a jump through time.

Then there are the people who seem to be able to willfully influence and control time. To some, this ability exhibits as ESP, prophecies and precognition. Others are able to experience the past much as we view the present. However, they are not able to interact with past events, they can only watch like they are seeing a movie or television show.

A few talented people have the power to physically travel between the walls of Time and Space. Not only are they able to cross over into the past or future, but they are also able to journey to other realities that conjoin with ours. These other realities or dimensions are the infinite possibilities that have branched out from the first reality of creation. Everything that can be, is. Every choice you make, every wish you have is made real in other possibilities. Of course some things are more possible than others. These possibilities are assessable to those who know what doorways to take.

Brad Steiger in his book **Strange Disappearances** tells about a letter he got from a man who claimed to be able to "see" the natural doorways that lead into other worlds and times. Not only was Al Kiessig able to see these entrances between realities, but he also had the ability to walk through into other dimensions.

Kiessig told Steiger that it was in Missouri that he found the "West Door," the door of evil, and the "East Door," the entrance into the Spirit World.

"At the West Door, the wanderers of the spirit world can leave and enter our world clothed so as to be seen as one of us -- and no human eye can detect the difference. There are two places, one in Missouri and one in Arkansas, where I walked into this next door world. It is very silent. It looks like our world, but there is no sound, no wind, no sun, even though it looks like the sun is shining.

"In the state of Missouri I found two fields that had doors, or what I call 'vortexes.' no matter where you walked you would come back to your starting place, and if you hit the center of the vortex, then you would come out from a mile to two miles beyond the place you entered, in a section that would be unrecognizable to you until you stopped and regained your inner balance. Then the surroundings would gradually become familiar."

Kiessig believes that each door is different, but that if he could recognize these openings, he or anyone else could pick a door and appear instantaneously anywhere at anytime in the universe.

"In December of 1965," says Kiessig, "my wife and I moved back to Arkansas. Shortly thereafter, I left the house about 9:30 AM to walk with my dog along two sides of a 40-acre field. I walked to the corner directly opposite the house up on the side of a steep hill. From that corner to the road was 3/4's of one side of the 40-acre square, and as it took me about 45 minutes to get to that corner, there was no reason why I should not have been back to the house before noon.

"So I started walking along the fence. I walked up one hill and down another, paying no attention to anything but the fence. Then I stopped to rest and my dog came to me. From then on, he stayed

Time Travel – Fact Not Fiction

close to my side, which was odd for him. I was walking slowly, since I have emphysema and I have no wind to speak of. Then I noticed the quiet. No shadows. No wind. I said to myself that I would walk to the top of the hill so that I could see just where I was.

"When I finally reached the top, I saw a fenced-in hayfield. Less than 3/4's of a mile away there were two wooden-frame, two-story houses. Each house had the usual accumulation of stuff in the yards, but there were no cars or garages.

"There was a mud or gravel road in front of each house. One house appeared to me to be facing south with a road running east and west. The other house was facing me with a road running north and south. These roads did not connect.

"There was no sign of life. There was no smoke from the chimneys. All this time Joe, my dog, stood there looking at me. So when I said, 'Let's go back the way we came,' he was one happy dog.

"It wasn't until we got to that strange corner that we felt the breeze and heard the crows and other birds. We were glad to be back. I walked to the house the short way, because I knew it would be about 12:30 PM, and I would be a half-hour late.

"When I was nearly to the house, I noticed that the winter sun was only about two hours from setting. I was amazed to see that the clock in the house said 3:30 PM."

Kiessig also mentions that in the region of the Ozarks, it was easy for him to see into other dimensions, even though he could not enter. He claimed that he could see the people who lived in these other worlds. People who entered our world both intentionally and unintentionally.

"Some of these doors to other dimensions open like an elevator door with no elevator there to step into. Others open into a land of no life. Some take you back into the past and some take you into the future of this world. I have entered these 'doorways' while driving and have saved myself hundreds of miles of driving. Unfortunately, the reverse has also happened to me."

Other people have reported the strange phenomena of "compressed time," trips that would normally take hours, unexpectedly taking only minutes. Could these people have also accidentally entered a doorway across Time and Space?

On fourteen different occasions between 1971 and 1972, while alone or with friends, Bill Nelson of Lockport, New York, traversed distances of up to 30 miles under extremely mysterious circumstances.

Time Travel – Fact Not Fiction

In each case Nelson was traveling in a car and somehow jumped from five to fifteen miles during each incident. As far as anyone who experienced the jumps could tell, no noticeable loss in time occurred during the jumps.

The first incident took place one night late in October 1971. With his son Willie, Nelson was driving from Burt, New York along Route 78 to Lockport. The pair stopped at a friend's home around 9:45 PM, but then continued at 10:00 PM.

As they drove toward Niagara Falls, they talked about the days events when they suddenly noticed they were nearing Nelson's parents' apartment. Nelson was surprised to see it so soon, but thought that he had merely lost track of time. They decided to drop in for a few minutes to say hi before going on home.

"While my mother fussed over my son, I talked with my father," remembered Nelson. "I noticed that his air-pressure clock showed exactly 10:00 PM. I remarked, 'Hey Dad, your clock's stopped.' 'It never stops,' he said while glancing at his wristwatch. 'It's just 10:01, right on the button.' Still not convinced, I looked at my watch. It indicated 10:03."

Bill and his son agreed that they had left their friend's home, about 22 miles away, at 10:00. However, they assumed that their friend's clock must have been wrong. How else could they explain how they covered 22 miles in less than a minute?

Three nights later Bill and his son were once again driving between Burt and Lockport. It was around midnight and both were extremely tired. All of a sudden Bill got the feeling that he was lost. The road ahead somehow didn't seem right. He realized that there was no hill between Burt and the town of Wright's Corners on 78, yet there was one right in front of them. Stunned, Bill pulled over and asked his son, "Willie, where are we?"

Bill's son told him what he already knew, but refused to accept. "Lockport hill," he said. "But Dad, it can't be. We didn't go through Wright's Corners or Newfane."

The two tried to trace the familiar road from Burt to the place they now were. They could remember nothing but a straight road, no right turn at the traffic light in Wright's Corners, no traveling down the main street nor the lights and thoroughfare through Newfane. Minutes before they had been in Burt, now they were twenty miles away. They were confused, but were certain that they had not been driving 120 miles an hour. A third incident that year served only to deepen the mystery. Late in October, Bill, his son and two friends—Robin DeVoe

Time Travel – Fact Not Fiction

and Dave Hughes left Lockport for the Olcott Yacht Club. Just as they started Bill noticed that his watch had stopped. He asked Dave what time he had. "Two-twenty-seven," he said. Bill set his watch, wound it and the four set out.

In just a few minutes they rounded a bend and saw the Yacht Club on their right. Trying to suppress his fear, Bill asked Dave again what time it was.

"Two-thirty-four," he replied. "Why? Did your watch stop again?"

"How far is it from Lockport to where we are now?" Bill asked his passengers.

"Seven to Wright's Corners," said Robin from the back seat, "about five or six to Newfand, another seven here. I'd say about 20 miles, give or take. Why?"

"How fast did we have to travel to cover 20 miles in seven minutes?" asked Bill.

"Holy cow," they all exclaimed and looking at their watches. "That's impossible. What the hell are you trying to pull?"

Later at the club, they sipped colas and discussed the impossible. None of us could recall passing through towns but Bill thought he could remember stopping for a light in Newfane. The others insisted he had not stopped along the way. Had the four all hallucinated? Or had they undergone a skip in time?

Bill experienced other time skips during 1972, always in the same area and usually when he was with his son or his friend Dave Hughes. The most startling incident took place when Bill was alone and found himself inexplicably turned around and headed back the way he had come, but on a different road.

The other skips of that year were less dramatic but just as puzzling. Still they did not compare with a terrifying experience Bill had in the early part of 1972.

That night, Bill was driving home from Lockport down a dark road. No other cars were anywhere in sight. He was doing about 50 miles an hour when all of a sudden, as if out of nowhere, a car backed out onto the highway in front of his car. There was no way to avoid the other car and Bill slammed on his brakes and skidded 50 feet into the cars right door. Fortunately no one was killed, although a woman was injured. Later the other driver claimed that just before he backed out of his driveway he had looked up and down the road, visibility was clear for half a mile, but had seen nothing.

Time Travel – Fact Not Fiction

"Then suddenly," he said, "this guy was right on top of me and before I could get out of the way he hit me."

After that incident Bill Nelson's time skips became fewer until they stopped altogether. Bill has often wondered if they would someday resume, so far they haven't, and that's all right with him.

Time Slows Down For A Runner

V. Fred Rayser was a teenage trackster. He had set a number of records in the 880 which made it his favorite event. He also ran the 440 and, when track season ended, ran cross country.

Rayser wrote in the August 1983 issue of *Fate* magazine that he had heard of distance runners going into a state of euphoria, but the 440 and the 880 are sprints that do not provide enough time to work-up into any kind of altered state, except for one strange occasion during the summer track season in 1937 which was forever burned into his memory.

In Spring Valley, New York, Rayser was competing in the First Annual Valkyrie Track and Field Championships. The weather was good, it was bright and sunny but not too hot.

Upon checking in Rayser discovered that the 880 was a handicap event, something he had never run before. In theory, the slower runners are given a head start so that, if the handicappers have figured correctly and right conditions prevail, all the runners will finish in a dead heat, photo finish.

Rayser writes that, "I got my handicap and was encouraged to see that I was given a 10-yard head start. I was encouraged until I took my starting position and discovered there was nobody behind me. I was the scratch man. Not only was everybody in front of me but some were almost out of sight

"There were about 15 runners in front of me and one was almost opposite me on the far side of the track. He was running a lap and a half while I had to run two laps. If it hadn't been for my cheering section, my dad and brother, I would have walked off the track."

Rayser's strategy was to pass as may runners as he could on the straightaways and managed to catch half the field. But as he was coming off the backstretch on the final lap, he could see seven runners still ahead of him. With only 100 yards to the finish line he knew he had to run wide around the "U" turn for half the distance in order to pass. He felt there was no hope in winning.

Time Travel – Fact Not Fiction

"Then it happened," said Rayser. "As I started around the curve, the light appeared to change from bright sunshine to a muted glow. It was as if I had suddenly entered into a translucent tunnel. I was conscious only of the runners ahead of me. Their legs were churning and their arms flailing but they seemed to be moving in slow motion.

"Not only that, but they were scattered all over the track instead of being grouped at the pole as is normal. Never before, or since, have I seen runners so dispersed. I began to weave my way through them. Some of the runners were taking the turn so wide that I easily passed them on the inside instead of having to run around them.

"Then, as I came off the curve, the light changed again. I emerged from the 'tunnel' into the bright sunshine with nothing ahead of me but the tape less than fifty yards away. I hit the tape at full speed and kept on going. I felt that I could run another lap or even two at the same pace. I gradually slowed down, however, and jogged the rest of the way around the track.

"My cheering section came out of the stands to pound me on the back and congratulate me on a record time. I was happy but thought it best not to mention my strange experience. With all of us sprinting for the finish, I had passed seven runners in fifty yards around a curve, an 'impossible' accomplishment.

"I picked up the gold medal but my mind was full of questions without answers. What was the change of light? Why were the other runners going in slow motion but not me? Had I hallucinated? What gave me so much energy that kept on running after I hit the finish line? Had I entered a time warp or another dimension? Almost half a century later, I still wonder what happened to me that day."

People From Nowhere

If people can consciously influence the Time and Space around them, what happens if this ability should occur spontaneously? Charles Fort tells in one of his books of a naked man who suddenly appeared on High Street, Chatham, Kent, England, on January 6, 1914. People walking on the same street gave witness that the man had quite literally appeared from nowhere. He was just suddenly there, confused, frightened and having no idea who he was or where he had come from.

In *Lo!*, Fort writes that six people were discovered wandering on the streets of the small town of Romford, Essex, England, between January 14, 1920 and December 9, 1923. None of these mentally

Time Travel – Fact Not Fiction

distraught individuals were able to tell how they had got there or anything else about themselves. It was a mystery that was never solved. Had these unfortunate people been accidentally transported through time to end up in a completely different era? Perhaps this is what happens to some of the thousands of people who vanish off the face of the Earth every year.

In 1953, a schoolteacher in Wellington, New Zealand, named H.F. North arrived in a London police station insisting that a hoax was the farthest thing from his mind. He simply wanted to go home, and he had no idea what on earth he was doing in London.

According to North, he had left his home one morning to walk to the school where he taught. The school was in Wellington, New Zealand. The next thing he knew, he told police, was that he was walking the streets of London, England. He had no idea how he got there, and he was further stunned to learn that he had lost four days in the process. However, North was certain that one moment he was in New Zealand and the next he was in London and four days in the future. He had literally walked into the future.

Is it any wonder then that the human mind would react adversely by the abruptness brought about by changes in Time and Space? One factor that seems to be almost universal with such traumatic time shifts is that the unwilling participants usually emerge with amnesia and other forms of mental disturbances. It's almost like the mind shuts down to protect itself from the completely unknown sensations caused by temporal displacement.

H.M. Cranmer of Hammersley Fork, Pennsylvania wrote to *Fate* magazine in November 1956 about a puzzling incident that happened when he was a schoolboy in 1897. According to Mr. Cranmer, an Irish immigrant lad named Thomas Eggleton left the home of his employer, Hamilton Fish, a farmer, to mail a letter at the country-store post office.

Tommy mailed his letter, bought a nickel's worth of candy and started for home. The next morning at 5:00 AM, a search was begun for the young man, who had never returned to his room or to the farm of his employer. His tracks were found leaving the general store and leading to the Kettle Creek bridge, there they stopped.

An extensive area search was continued for several days, and Mr. Cranmer could remember that the schools were closed for two weeks because pupils were afraid to walk to and from school.

Four years later the Boer War in South Africa had started. By then, Hamilton Fish had passed away never learning the fate of his employee. One day one of Mr. Fish's daughters received a letter

Time Travel – Fact Not Fiction

meant for her father. The letter was from Tommy and came from South Africa. Tommy had been wounded in the head and this had restored his memory. For four years he had lived in South Africa without knowing who he was or where he had came from. When the head wound restored his memory, the last thing he could recall was working for Mr. Fish in Pennsylvania. Tommy remained in South Africa, but he could offer no explanation on how he suddenly ended up there after leaving the country store in Pennsylvania four years previously.

Earlier in the chapter Al Kiessig wrote that he could see people from other realities enter our Universe from "doorways" in Time and Space. While some of these beings may be coming here voluntarily, others may be just as shocked to suddenly find themselves thrust into a completely different place...our world.

In a village near Frankfurt-am-Oder, Germany, in the summer of 1850, a man was found wandering around in a daze, completely surprised by his surroundings. He could with effort produce a few words of German and was at last able to explain to the authorities and to reporters that his name was Joseph Vorin, and that he had come from beyond the oceans from a nation named Laxaria in Sakria. This was fine except for one thing, Laxaria did not exist, at least in this universe.

French newspapers reported the case of a strange young man who, on September 17, 1905, was charged as a vagrant. The charge was no doubt as meaningless to the young man as were his words to the Paris police. The young man spoke a tongue which no linguist, Asian, or specialists in African dialects could interpret. Did this man also come from the country of Laxaria?

A British sailor by the name of Charles Jamison somehow ended up in the emergency ward of the U.S. Public Health Service Hospital in Boston. This in itself is not so unusual, however, upon further investigation, Charles Jamison appeared to have been an unwilling visitor to our world.

On February 11 1945 at 2:20 AM an unmarked, blue ambulance arrived without warning and dropped off an injured man into the hospital's emergency ward. "You will call this man Charles Jamison," said the driver as he left.

The duty nurse later remembered that she had never seen the driver before, plus he was oddly dressed. "He was strange," she said. "He wore a dark overcoat. I think it had brass buttons, not like a policeman's, more like a coat worn by on officer on a ship."

Time Travel – Fact Not Fiction

The new patient had been badly injured. He was comatose with bluish-white sores and skin lacerations. Jamison was also suffering from ostcomyelitis, a bone disease and appeared to have suffered a stroke. His back and legs were covered with infected shrapnel wounds. His cheek revealed a two-inch scar that had been stitched by an amateur. On his left hand, the index finger had been chopped off below the middle joint.

Jamison would survive his injuries, but it was obvious that he was also suffering from some kind of mental trauma. He would or could not talk and he spent his time in a wheelchair, staring out the window. The doctors could not determine if his silence was from his stroke or by psychological trauma.

Months went by with no luck in finding any relatives or records to verify that their patient was named Charles Jamison. Fingerprints were sent to each branch of the armed forces, the Merchant Marines, and the FBI. All reported negative results. This was extremely puzzling to officials due to Jamison's elaborate tattoos. Both arms presented crossed American and British flags and interlocking hearts. The words "U.S. Navy" were clearly seen under the American flag; "United" was under the English flag, but another word that could have been "Kingdom" was faded.

After many months of silence, Charles Jamison suddenly began to speak. What he told the astonished doctors, however, only deepened the mystery of his origin. Hospital Director Dr. Oliver C. Williams was a nautical scholar and he was determined to find out the identity of his strange patient.

Dr. Williams' examination began with a series of questions designed to explore Jamison's subconscious in an attempt to reveal his past. Jamison seemed to have an amazing knowledge of historical events, especially military history. Dr. Williams believed that Jamison was a sailor and one day asked him "What time did you sail, Charles?"

Jamison turned around and answered: "We cleared the harbor and moved south by southeast. It must have been after midnight, by your time."

Dr. Williams was now convinced that Jamison had been a sailor. Over the next few weeks, Williams showed Jamison illustrations of British ships and military uniforms. Jamison was able to correctly identify them and even pointed out mistakes that were later confirmed by military experts. Jamison also claimed to have been in the Royal Navy ammunition depot in London. However, the building no longer existed. Jamison would to have been more than 80 years old to have been in the building, and he was no more than fifty years old. Jamison had another surprise as he spoke about the naval gunnery school in Gosport in 1850. He vividly described the weapons, ships, number of men, and the restricted areas inside the school. All of these revelations were confirmed by Alton Barker, chief of the British Information Service.

When the investigation was concluded, Jamison had claimed to have served on the British battleship, **HMS Bellerophon** and said that he had been on board during the Battle of Jutland on May 31, 1916. Jamison also said that he had last served on the three-masted clipper **Cutty Sark**, which had been launched in 1869.

A newspaper article about the lost sailor at the Boston hospital caught the attention of a Merchant Marine officer who had formally served aboard a troop transport. He told Dr. Williams to check out the manifest for the **USS Lejeune** because he seemed to remember a man named Jamison.

A U.S. Immigration and Naturalization Service investigator found a notation in the official documents of the **USS Lejeune**. The ship's manifest said that Charles Jamison had been picked up at sea, time unknown. He was assigned to the Lejeune's manifest out of Southampton, England, on January 24 1945, and arrived in Boston on February 9, 1945.At the bottom was written: "Charles William Jamison, July 17, 1895, Boston Mass. Catholic, four years in a German POW camp in Belgium."

Oddly, the information about Jamison had been handwritten on the manifest. Normally, the Lejeune's manifest was properly typed and signed by the ship's officers. The Lejeune's former captain was surprised but unable to offer an explanation. It was against procedure to handwrite names on a prepared roster. He was certain that the handwritten portion about Jamison had not been there when the transport sailed from Southampton.

Official checks by the Bureau of Vital Statistics going back to 1890 showed no evidence that a Charles William Jamison ever existed. However, Dr. Williams had requested a history of the **Cutty Sark** from Lloyd's Register of Ships. When this arrived, it contained an odd attachment from the log of a German submarine. According to the German High Command, the crew of the U-24 was astonished to see an ancient three-masted clipper ship when they surfaced on the morning of July 10 1941. Gilded letters on the ship's bow read **Cutty Sark**.

An order was given for the ship to stand by and be boarded, but the vessel turned away. Minutes later the sub sent a torpedo cutting into the ship, sending it quickly to the ocean floor. The submarine's crew saw a few bodies and pulled a sole survivor from the sea. That man, named Charles William Jamison, was taken to a German port and then transferred to a German POW camp in Belgium.

No one could explain how Charles Jamison could have been aboard a sailing ship that had not been at sea in more than 20 years. In addition, no one knew how the official German report found its way into the Lloyd's document in the first place. And no one could explain how the **Cutty Sark** could be torpedoed by a German U-boat when she had spent the entire war at a dock in Greenhithe, England.

Charles Jamison spent the remainder of his life at the Boston hospital. He died on January 19, 1975. No record was ever found confirming the identity of the unknown sailor who may have found himself lost forever from the world he once knew.

If people can consciously influence the Time and Space around them, what happens if this ability should occur spontaneously?

Chapter Six
The Philadelphia Experiment

No book about time travel would be complete without at least a brief mention of the infamous Philadelphia Experiment and the subsequent stories, rumors and myths that blossomed out of that first letter written by the elusive Carlos Allende to UFO author Morris K. Jessup.

The genesis of the Philadelphia Experiment myth dates back to 1955 with the publication of ***The Case for UFO's*** by the late Morris K. Jessup. Some time after the publication of the book, Jessup received correspondence from a Carlos Miguel Allende, who gave his address as R.D. #1, Box 223, New Kensington, Pa.

In his correspondence, Allende commented on Jessup's book and gave details of an alleged secret naval experiment conducted by the Navy in Philadelphia in 1943. During the experiment, according to Allende, a ship was rendered invisible and teleported to and from Norfolk in a few minutes, with some terrible aftereffects for crew members. Supposedly, this incredible feat was accomplished by applying Einstein's "unified field" theory.

Allende claimed that he had witnessed the experiment from another ship and that the incident was reported in a Philadelphia newspaper. In 1956 a copy of Jessup's book was mailed anonymously to ONR. The pages of the book were interspersed with handwritten comments which alleged a knowledge of UFOs, their means of motion, the culture and ethos of the beings occupying the UFOs, described in pseudoscientific and incoherent terms.

Two officers, then assigned to ONR, took a personal interest in the book and showed it to Jessup. Jessup concluded that the writer of those comments on his book was the same person who had written him about the Philadelphia Experiment. These two officers personally had the book retyped and arranged for the reprint, in typewritten form, of 25 copies. From this, the entire controversy surrounding the Philadelphia Experiment continued to grow as new information and rumors were added to the original story. In the 1980s new accounts of

Time Travel – Fact Not Fiction

the experiments began to surface. According to men like Al Bielek, the Philadelphia Experiment achieved not only invisibility and teleportation, but also the unexpected transference of the ship and its test crew across the time barrier. From these frightening beginnings the United States military was allegedly able to successfully perfect time travel at a secret location at the Montauk base on Long Island.

Although no official information has ever been uncovered proving conclusively that The Philadelphia Experiment was ever conducted, it is believed that the experiment had its genesis as far back as the 1930's. Research was conducted on the nature of electromagnetics and invisibility at the University of Chicago around 1931 or 1932 under the guidance of Dr. John Hutchinson Sr., who was Dean of the University, Nikola Tesla, and Dr. Kurtenaur, an Austrian physicist who was on staff. In 1933, the Institute of Advanced Studies at Princeton was formed and the Chicago University project was transferred there in 1934. One of the people on staff at the Institute was Dr. John Erich Von Neumann, who was from Budapest Hungary. Other people at the Institute included Albert Einstein, who left Germany in 1930. He taught at the California Institute of Technology for three years and then went to the Institute upon their invitation.

In 1935, Nikola Tesla became director of the invisibility project. In 1936, with his assistance, scientists achieved some partial invisibility in the laboratory. The Navy was encouraged to continue the work and supplied money for additional research. Unfortunately, Tesla was forced to resign from the project after being struck by a cab in 1937.

In 1940, after research using Tesla's approach, scientists decided they were ready for a full test at the Brooklyn Navy Yard. They had a small ship and a tender ship at each side. One ship provided the power and the other supplied the drive for the coils. They were tendered to the test ship by cables. The idea was that if anything went wrong they could cut the cables or sink the test ship. Everything worked and the project was declared a success.

The important point about the 1940 test is that there was no one on board the test vehicle. It was strictly a dry run with no people. This is significant because of what happened later.

With this success, the Navy decided to give the project unlimited funds and to classify the project. Even though Nikola Tesla had to resign as Director of the project, due to his injuries in 1937, he was still able to act as an consultant from his Manhattan hotel room. It was Dr. Von Neumann, however, who was the onsite director of the project. In 1942, the Navy gave Von Neumann a ship and a crew for a full sized test. Tesla and Von Neumann, however, did not see eye-to-eye about certain aspects concerning the upcoming test. Tesla insisted that the high-frequency electromagnetic fields posed an unknown danger to the test subjects onboard.

Tesla had such a run-in with the unexpected nature of electromagnetic fields in 1895. At that time, Tesla was experimenting with highly charged, rotating magnetic fields when he was accidently struck by an arc of almost 3.5 million volts of electricity. Tesla, on contact with the resonating electromagnetic charge, found himself outside his time-frame reference. He reported that he could see the immediate past - present and future, all at once. But he was paralyzed within the electromagnetic field, unable to help himself. His assistant, by turning off the current, released Tesla before any permanent damage was done.

Tesla insisted more time was needed to insure the safety of the human test subjects. However, the Navy, pressed by the expanding war in the Pacific, wouldn't agree. At the last moment, Tesla requested that the equipment be re-tuned to cover new parameters, knowing that this would result in sabotaging the test. After the failure of the 1940 test, Tesla resigned for good, leaving Von Neumann in charge.

Von Neumann requested additional time from the Navy to study what had gone wrong. He decided a special ship that was designed from the ground up would be needed. The USS Eldridge was selected for the experiment and while the ship was under construction, special preparations were made to have Tesla-based technology installed into the ship.

Supposedly four massive generator banks and modified Tesla coils were used to convert direct-current electricity to an alternating current and to step up the frequencies. As the steady current of electricity was harmonically increased with the help of a prototype of the UNIVAC computer, a magnetic field would envelop the ship. It has been said that despite Tesla's detailed instructions, shortcuts were taken. For example, instead of laying all the cable deep within the hull of the ship, they were instead laid along the outer walls. This may have contributed to the disaster that would soon follow.

After the ship was out of dry dock, thirty-three volunteers for the crew were assigned to the Eldridge. On July 22 1943, the first test was conducted. The test was a complete success and the ship became radar and optically invisible. They discovered, however, that the crew became very disoriented and suffered from unknown illnesses. The Navy pulled the crew off and consulted Von Neumann, who requested more time to try and determine just what exactly was going on physically with the crew. This was a new science and no one knew

Time Travel – Fact Not Fiction

the reasons for the unexplained side-effects. The Navy, after consultation with higher-ups, announced that the drop dead date would be August 12 1943. Von Neumann voiced his concern that this date did not give them enough opportunity to work out all of the bugs.

At this point, the Navy decided that it just wanted radar invisibility and not optical invisibility, so Von Neumann was forced to make quick modifications of the equipment. August 12 arrived and the test began, and for about a minute everything seemed to be working perfectly. The USS Eldridge became transparent but ships' outline could be seen in the water. There was suddenly a blue flash and the ship disappeared entirely. No radio communication was possible. It had completely disappeared. In about three hours it suddenly reappeared. One of the masts was broken and some personnel were partially embedded in the steel deck. Others were fading in and out of visibility. Some disappeared entirely never to be seen again.

Many of the crewmen suffered from unexplained and terrible mental disabilities. Interestingly enough, the same symptoms have been reported with people who have experienced "natural" time distortions. The Navy extracted the crew and went on with four days of meetings to decide what to do about the problem. They decided there would be one more test with another dry run without personnel.

They conducted the dry run using about one thousand feet of cable attached to another ship. In late October 1943 the test occurred. The ship disappeared for about twenty minutes. When it returned, they found equipment missing. Two transmitter cabinets and one generator were missing. The cabinet with the zero-time reference generator was intact. At that point, the Navy stripped the ship and stopped the project. The Eldridge, with a new crew, served in the war and was eventually turned over to Greece in 1951.

Books such as the **Montauk Project** have asserted that the Philadelphia Experiment resulted in the first successful, although unexpected, jump in Time and Space. A retired U.S. Marine writing for the February 1997 issue of *Fate* magazine under the name of Drue, claimed that he was one of the thirty-three volunteers on the Eldridge.

Drue claims that the crew was unable to deal with the physical trauma that overwhelmed them. They were paralyzed by fear and a powerful energy field. The ship and its crew were fragmented into different dimensions and magnetically pulled through Time and Space. The initial surge shot them from the Atlantic in 1943, to Niagara Falls in approximately 3543AD. Two of the ship's generator banks were destroyed by fire. Because of this they started to bounce uncontrollably across time like a rock skipping across a pond. To those on board, time ceased to exist. To some, their movement from place to place seemed to take hours. In some cases, the movement seemed to occur instantly. And at times, their existence on the ship seemed to last for an eternity.

"We traveled to a number of locations," writes Drue, "including the Norfolk Naval Base in 1944, the Armistad Reservoir in 1954 Texas, Arizona's Lake Powell in 1966, Chicago in 1969, New Mexico's Navajo Reservoir in 1977, and Nevada's Lake Mead in 1983."

While this story is interesting, there is no evidence that it is true. In fact, most of the wilder claims of time travel did not surface until after the release of the 1984 movie *The Philadelphia Experiment*. In fact, the originator of the entire affair, Carlos Miguel Allende, turned out to be a man named Carl M. Allen. Allen has corresponded over the years with a number of researchers such as Jacques Vallee and Loren Coleman. Loren has publicly stated that he believes that Allen suffers from mental problems.

Robert Goerman, in a 1980 issue of *Fate*, wrote that Carl Allen was a "master leg-puller." Allen's family showed Goerman letters in which "Allende" said he had made up the whole Philadelphia Experiment story.

Personnel at the Fourth Naval District believe that the questions surrounding the Philadelphia Experiment arose from quite routine research which occurred during World War II at the Philadelphia Naval Shipyard. Until recently, it was believed that the foundation for the stories arose from degaussing experiments which have the effect of making a ship undetectable or "invisible" to magnetic mines.

Another likely genesis of the bizarre stories about levitation, teleportation and effects on human crew members might be attributed to experiments with the generating plant of a destroyer, the USS Timmerman. In the 1950's this ship was part of an experiment to test the effects of a small, high-frequency generator providing 1,000 Hz instead of the standard 400hz. The higher frequency generator produced corona discharges, and other well known phenomena associated with high frequency generators. None of the crew suffered effects from the experiment.

This is not to say that there is not some validity in the Philadelphia Experiment scenario. With any rumor there are always some small grains of truth. It should also be remembered that secret projects during WWII were highly compartmentalized with only a few key people privy to the entire operation. The Manhattan Project is a good example of such secret operations. It is doubtful that in 1943 the level of understanding needed to rip open a hole in Time and Space even existed. Such a knowledge of physics and the effects of high-energy electromagnetic fields on the environment is still only theoretical. It is difficult to believe that scientists, who at the time, were still laboring to discover how to split the atom could have managed to send a ship shooting across the time barrier, even by accident.

Whatever happened to the USS Eldridge and its unfortunate crew will probably never be fully disclosed. The research conducted at that time undoubtedly continued afterwards under different project names. Unlike the Atomic bomb, the type of science developed from the Philadelphia Experiment is more subtle and certainly easier to keep under wraps.

A direct result of what was learned from the Philadelphia Experiment could have been what in now known as the Montauk Project. Made popular by a series of books: *The Montauk Project* (1992), *Montauk Revisited: Adventures In Synchronicity* (1994), *Pyramids of Montauk: Explorations In Consciousness* (1995), *The Black Sun: Montauk's Nazi-Tibetan Connection* (1997), and *Montauk: The Alien Connection* by Stewart Swerdlow with Peter Moon (editor) published in 1998, and all written by Preston Nichols and Peter Moon, the Montauk Project has achieved a small degree of notoriety among hard-core believers. Claiming a direct connection to the Philadelphia Experiment, the Montauk Project tells a disturbing story of a secret government gone wild, fantastic exotic technologies and the manipulation of time.

The Montauk Project

According to Preston Nichols and Peter Moon, after a series of crashed flying saucers in New Mexico and other parts of the world, the government decided that they needed to set up a series of bases to investigate this phenomena and find personnel that could decode the salvaged equipment by reverse engineering.

The Montauk Project was to be an elite black project investigating paranormal, psychic, and unconventional sciences. It was to include the most intelligent respected scientists in the world using the most sophisticated advanced computer equipment available. The Montauk Project allegedly became a huge project branching off into many other smaller projects including mind control, telepathy, teleportation, and time travel. The Montauk Project supposedly made its headquarters at the site known as Camp Hero, or the Montauk Air

Time Travel – Fact Not Fiction

Force Station which was originally commissioned by the U.S. Army in 1942. The site was chosen because of the fear of a New York invasion that might be staged from the sea. It was a coastal defense station that was disguised as a fishing village.

Camp Hero was named after Maj. Gen. Andrew Hero Jr., who was the Army's commander of coastal artillery. He died in 1942. Flanking the small housing development were two large concrete bunkers that were half-submerged beneath several feet of topsoil. The walls and ceilings of these bunkers were made of concrete that were over three feet thick.

Four 16 inch Naval guns were housed in these bunkers that faced the sea. They were to be used against any enemy craft that might attempt a landing there. The guns were never fired, and there was never any battle over Camp Hero during World War II. In 1947, the guns were dismantled by the Army and the metal was salvaged for scrap uses.

In 1950, the U.S. Air Force moved some personnel and equipment to the site and began radar surveillance operations. During this period, the base was run under a joint residence of the Army and Air Force, this continued until 1957. The army had set up some anti-aircraft batteries on the base to complement the radar equipment used by the Air Force. However, they were never fired.

The Army withdrew from Camp Hero in 1957 and removed the anti-aircraft batteries that it housed there. After the departure of the Army, the base was remained by the Defense Department as the Montauk Air Force Station.

In 1962, a huge five story cubical tower was commissioned that housed a gigantic 75ft. radar dish. Various other buildings on the site were also used for housing radar equipment-notably the "pink" or "orange" building as it has come to be called. These other buildings were the octagonal structures that remain today.

The Montauk Air Force Station continued to operate through the 1970's, the stage radar being used as a coastal defense warning system, and it employed both military, and civilian personnel. The Air Force itself submitted a proposal to the Carter Administration to close the base in 1978 as it had for the most part become obsolete, and continuous operation of the base was unnecessary.

The base was planned to close in July of 1981. The Reagan Administration had planned to retire the national debt by selling off surplus Federal land that wasn't being used. Camp Hero fell within these boundaries, and the GSA was given the task of disposing of it.

Time Travel – Fact Not Fiction

The base would continue to operate in compliance with the FAA as a ground to air radio station until 1982, with a military staff of five.

As of today, the Montauk Air Force Station still exists, however it is a derelict facility. The houses, radar buildings and the bunkers are all still there but are in a serious state of disrepair and decay. Left at the mercy of time and vandalism, they have become crumbled relics of the past.

The entirety of Camp Hero has since been donated to New York State as a state park but the portions of the inner base containing the buildings and other structures is off limits to the public—it is a potentially hazardous site for casual strollers as it is believed that chemical weapons testing had been conducted on the grounds sometime in the 1950s. This site has also become infamous to those who believe that Montauk is the home of Project Phoenix.

Project Phoenix

Project Phoenix was supposedly the follow-up research for Project Rainbow, or the Philadelphia Experiment. This research, located at Brookhaven National Laboratories (Long Island, NY), was lead by Dr. John von Neumann. The objective of Project Phoenix was to find out how the human mind works and why people could not be subjected to inter-dimensional phenomena without complications.

Dr. von Neumann allegedly used a vast database of Nazi psychological research that the allies had confiscated after the war. With these resources Dr. von Neumann attempted to couple computer technology with sophisticated radio equipment in an attempt to link people's minds with machines. Dr. von Neumann succeeded to a point where he had made a virtual mind reading machine. The technology was also adapted so a psychic could think a thought and it could potentially affect the mind of another person, no matter how far away they were. The alleged discoveries involving mind/machine melding had alarming potentials.

Project Phoenix obtained a superior knowledge of the workings of the human mind, it also opened up the possibility of human mind control. When a full report was submitted to Congress, they ordered the project disbanded for the fear of having their own minds controlled.

After Congress ordered the project disbanded, several private groups attempted to influence the military with the idea that this technology could be used to control an enemy's mind during warfare.

Time Travel – Fact Not Fiction

Finally, a secret group with sufficient financial resources and a tie with the military decided to set up a research facility at Camp Hero. They made this choice based on the fact that the base contained a large Sage radar antenna which emitted a frequency of about 400-425 Megahertz (Coincidentally the same band used to enter the human mind).

Camp Hero was reactivated during the late 1960s and by 1972, the Montauk Project was fully operation. Massive mind control experiments began on humans, and any other animal deemed to have consciousness. Over a few years, the Montauk researchers had perfected mind control techniques and continued to study the far reaches of human potential.

By developing the psychic ability of some of the personnel, they eventually came to the point where they could amplify the psychic's thoughts. During this amplification, the psychics could create matter and manifest illusions. Through further study and the hypothesis that one could bend time itself, the Montauk project opened the first controlled time portal.

The Montauk project finally reached the climax in which they opened a time vortex back to 1943 and the original Philadelphia Experiment. The Montauk Project came to an end when a man named Duncan Cameron, who was a psychic guinea pig, was taken out to Camp Hero. Duncan was the primary psychic used for the time travel experiments, he was also present aboard the USS Eldridge during the original Philadelphia Experiment.

The Montauk Project supposedly came to an end on August 12 1983. The project by that time had created a fully operational time portal, but things were getting out of hand. Duncan called together a group of people who decided to crash the project. While sitting in the Montauk Chair (A device connected to esoteric radio receivers studded with crystals that sent thoughts out of a giant transmitter), Duncan unleashed a giant beast from within his subconscious which literally destroyed the project. The people who had been working on the base suddenly abandoned it. The air shafts and entrances to the major underground facilities were filled with cement and the lower levels, filled with water.

In its heyday, Preston Nichols says that the Montauk Project was on the cutting edge of quantum physics research. It is this aspect which led another person to dig into the underworld of Camp Hero. "There is solid scientific basis for what Nichols said in his books," writes John A. Quinn, who was also prompted to write on the Camp Hero saga.

Time Travel – Fact Not Fiction

"This is not a joke to me," said Quinn. "Electromagnetically, you can wipe the slate clean and implant false memories activated by radio frequency signals to trigger alternate states of mind. The phenomenon is called 'psychotronics' and direct hookups have been demonstrated on television. The real state of the art, however, is kept top-secret and is years beyond what is currently believed."

Since about 1988, New York State has been conducting a cleanup of the old Air Force Station, but Nichols and Quinn claim this story is false. Large drums, said to contain oil, were taken out of underground storage facilities recently. Asbestos wrapped around aboveground water main pipes connecting the houses in the village, however, has yet to be removed.

"You can't touch asbestos in the open air without a protective suit," said Nichols. "That should have been the first thing done. The base is still operational in secret underground facilities. There is no telling what kind of activity is currently being done. But radio signals being intercepted out of the area lead me to believe that the time travel and interdimensional projects are still being conducted to this very day."

As with the Philadelphia Experiment—the Montauk Project has become so muddled with myths and rumors that it has become impossible to separate fact from fiction. In fact, the amount of disinformation that has been spread over the years about the Montauk Project leads me to believe that some kind of secret project was conducted at the base. However, the true nature of the project has been effectively hidden by wild stories that have grown stranger with each new book.

Are the stories about time machines and exotic technologies simply wild fabrications of Intelligence operatives who are trying to hide more mundane military projects? Or have there been actual technological advances in the science of physics and time travel? There are people who now claim that they have uncovered the secrets of time and have constructed working machines to prove their allegations.

Chapter Seven
Time Machines

A working time machine has been the focus of countless science fiction novels, movies and television shows. The idea is that science and technology can solve the greatest challenge put before humankind: To be able to build a machine that can send its operator back into the past, or forwards to the future. Unfortunately, science fact is still somewhat disheartening to those who dream of hunting dinosaurs or watching the pyramids in Egypt being built.

Most scientists scoff at the idea of building a functional time machine. The physicists who are brave enough to attempt a study of the complexities of time travel cannot agree if the concept is even theoretically possible. At this point, our understanding of Time and Space is not sufficient to go beyond mere speculation.

However, there are people who say that time machines can now be built using technology that is available in any electronics store. Are these claims of working time machines true? Or do they still only exist in the imaginations of science fiction writers.

The popular website Keelynet has received quite a few e-mails speculating on the theories of time travel. An e-mail, received on January 31 1994, goes beyond the realm of speculation and tells about an accidental discovery made by a electronic tinkerer.

John Bajak of White Plains, New York wrote that he had just built an electroshock machine made of batteries, a capacitor, and a switch. But, just by chance, he decided to attach to the leads of the machine a piezoelectric crystal.

"The air turned funny when I pressed the button," said Bajak.

"I could see and feel an effect I can only describe as an electrical and subliminally acoustical roller coaster. At first it gave me headaches. I brought it to a pizza place where I used to work and sprayed their foyer. It gave them a headache too. I noticed time stretched thinner until I noticed it seemed to stop while the machine was turned on. This took place in clocks on my VCR and a German made clock. I noticed time seemed to decelerate after a certain period of turn on, then accelerate when the button was turned off, according to the changing pattern of the capacitor.

Bajak realized that he had built a "flux capacitor." A term made popular from the movie Back to the Future. But Bajak thought the term was fitting and went ahead and used it for his device. Bajak came up with a way that it could be attached to any internal combustion engine, and how in a static frame could be extremely dangerous. He finally decided that it could be used for time travel.

Unfortunately, John Bajak began to experience unusual problems in the form of exploding television sets and increasing paranoia. Bajak attributed these circumstances to his use of the flux capacitor. He felt that some group, possibly government or military, who was also involved in time experiments, was aware of his findings and wanted to stop him.

Finally after a series of phone calls to the police, Bajak found himself committed to the Florida North Psychiatric Hospital. Despite his problems, Bajak continues his research into what he now calls the "Bajak Circuit." By making the designs available on the Internet, Bajak is also encouraging others to try their own experiments in an attempt to verify his initial findings.

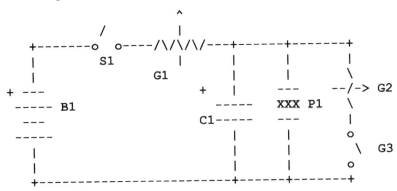

B1 27 volt source
C1 1200 uF 50V electrolytic
P1 piezoelectric transducer (value uncritical)
S1 charging switch (SPST)
G1 25-ohm rheostat (future control)
G2,G3 switch (SPST) and 1M-ohm potentiometer for past control

(Transcriber's note: I don't know whether G1 and G2 are really supposed to be a rheostat and a potentiometer, or both rheostats, or both pots. He refers to two rheostats elsewhere, and I was just going to call them pots until I remembered that rheostats would have some inductance.)

TO THE CHRONAUT - READ THIS MANUAL!

Instructions for Use of Temporal Flux Generator:

With batteries installed,

Depress switch for 3 to 4 seconds,

Release for 3 to 4 seconds;

Repeat as necessary.

IMPORTANT! Point transducer output toward the person or thing you want changed. That thing, such as a clock or piece of shelving, will begin oscillating between past and future.

Depending on which side of time you catch it on, depending also on the periods of switch on/off, and direction pointed, creates action, derived from oscillating time. DANGER! Do Not point at yourself for any appreciable amount of cycles. Damage to your time detection circuits may occur, damaging your overall sanity. You may in the course of activation, meet yourself. Do not panic; be reassured that if you know yourself, only one of you will survive.

The generator is more powerful during nighttime. If directed toward yourself at night, do not be surprised if you cannot sleep. However, try to sleep. The process of sleep reintegrates you. If at all possible, "SLEEP!"

Daytime may bring observations of being darker than day usually is. Direct Sunlight Radiation is good for burning off disintegration, but communication of time travel existence is an effect that others may not believe or can comprehend.

Another interesting letter from Keelynet came from the Emanon Inventors Association. The letter relates a fascinating story about a device called a caduceus coil.

"Well, it started last year around the middle of October when a friend of mine decided to build a shortwave receiver for his stepson as a Christmas gift. About a week, or so, after he finished his son's radio, he decided to build a radio for himself. However, he didn't want just any old radio, he wanted a full-wave/full-frequency radio.

"To save on verbosity, I won't go into the construction with much detail. However, I will say that the design could produce extremely high frequencies (to include the electromagnetic spectrum of light). I don't think we realized that at the time the radio was being built. But after studying schematics of assorted magnetrons (after the temporal displacements), we realized that this radio could go into that wavelength region. It is interesting to note that Nikola Tesla was quoted as saying that by producing a 'wall of light' (no doubt with electromagnetic energy) space and time could be manipulated.

"One night he was fiddling with the radio for the better part of a late-night/early morning jaunt. That particular night (well, actually the early morning hours of the next day) it was raining and there was a local electrical storm in progress.

"About 3:00AM, all of a sudden, the loudspeaker of his radio started making this God-awful obnoxiously loud noise. Since he was living in an apartment, he immediately cut the speaker leads to the speaker so as not to bother his next-door neighbors. Once that was done, he whipped out his multimeter and started taking voltage checks of the circuitry. To his amazement, he was getting 44 - 45-volts D.C. circuit wide (the radio was built to run off of 18 Volts D.C.).

"We talked about this afterwards and came to the conclusion that the aerial was inducting lots of highly-ionized air (from the rain and electrical storm) and thereby stepping up the voltage into the radio. It is of interest that John Bajak, developer of the Bajak Time Travel Flux Capacitor, claims his device operates on 44 Volts D.C.

"About five minutes to four in the morning, and still taking voltage checks, my friend received a rather pronounced static discharge from the radio. He stepped back and noticed that, just above the coils, was a very peculiar glowing electrical field just above the center of the coils. He mentioned that this anomaly appeared completely circular with 3-4 glowing blue bands of light separated by bands of space. The space in between the glowing bands seemed to be pulsating from complete transparency to semi-opaqueness.

"We attributed this phenomenon (the pulsations) to electromagnetic 'needles'(another concept that is too complex to be described right now). We thought this field might be one of two things: (1) - St. Elmo's Fire (we dismissed this because this phenomenon glows with more of a purplish color and certainly doesn't cause complete circular, band delimited, glowing). (2) - Electrical ionization of nitrogen

Time Travel – Fact Not Fiction

(also dismissed because nitrogen doesn't glow blue or produce completely circular fields). This glowing field lasted about six - seven seconds and, then, abruptly disappeared. The most amazing thing, though, was the fact that after this field disappeared, all the clocks in his apartment had moved from 3:55AM to 10:00PM.

"In fact, he then was able to use his 'radio' to tune in our one, and only, local radio station (1450 KONP in Port Angeles, WA) and was just in time to hear the beginning of the Ten o'clock news broadcast from the night before. He spent the rest of his 'additional' six hours taking voltage/current checks on his radio. The multimeter was reading about 18 Volts D.C. (normal operational voltage).

"About 3:00AM, again, the voltage levels shot up to 44 - 45 Volts D.C. and precisely at 3:55AM, again, this weird glowing electrical field appeared. This time, however, I guess he must have been expecting it to appear and, almost as soon as it appeared, he ripped out the aerial wire. This caused the glowing field to immediately disappear and he guesses that it was probably present, this time, for about one to two seconds.

"This time the clocks all jumped from 3:55AM to 2:30AM. He tuned in KONP again, and right around 2:45 heard the radio announcer announce the time as '2:45AM here at our station.' A few minutes after that, he unplugged his radio, got drunk, and fell asleep.

"Later that day, sometime in the afternoon, he said one of his next-door neighbors came over to ask him if he was working with any radio-transmission equipment because his friend was watching T.V., with his AM radio on low volume, a few minutes before four that morning when the reception on both his T.V. and radio went completely screwy for about six - seven seconds. WEIRD!

"When he first told me of this tale, I thought he was just so much full of you- know-what. However, for months after that he bought every book he could find on electromagnetics and electrodynamics and was studying these texts for hours per day. So, maybe something really did happen. The one thing that puzzled both of us is that he did not meet a chronologically younger (six hours) version of himself after the first displacement and did not meet a chronologically younger (about one and a half hour) version of himself after the second displacement.

"We pondered on this for months. Finally, we found a book entitled **Black Holes And Time Warps - Einstein's Outrageous Legacy** (by Kip Thorne) which seems to have answered that perplexing question. In the book, it mentions theories which seem to come close to what happened to my friend. In the book the authors

Time Travel – Fact Not Fiction

talk about what is known as an 'electromagnetic stretch.' When I read this it seemed very similar to the bizarre effects that happened to him. They hypothesize that the universe oscillates (electromagnetically at certain fundamental, and harmonic, frequencies) not only in three dimensions but in TIME as well and that if you could shield yourself from these oscillations, using counter-oscillating magnetic fields, that it might be possible to arrive at different times. They do mention that we are not aware of this process because we oscillate along with the universe and, therefore, never notice these oscillating time shifts.

"I have heard that what my friend accidentally built (and later called a 'caduceus coil'), is actually a tensor coil, invented by Wilbert Brockhouse Smith sometime during the 1950's (Smith died in 1961). Originally, Dr. Smith was involved in the top-secret program Project Magnet. This project, allegedly, was a government sponsored program to produce an aircraft which operated on the same propulsion/flight principles of UFOs. Smith was tinkering around with new styles of coil windings. It was during this period of time when he developed the caduceus coil.

"The coil is said to produce electromagnetic waves which travel parallel to the coil windings. This violates electromagnetic convention as the standard rule for creating electromagnetism is that the waves are produced perpendicularly (with respect to the coil windings). Supposedly, a caduceus coil transmits these electromagnetic waves at super-luminal velocities (i.e., at faster than light speeds).

"It is interesting to note that recently a Canadian scientist was credited with sending a radio broadcast using 'radio-like waves' which were traveling faster than the speed of light. Smith claimed that timepieces, which were within the caduceus coil's region of greatest magnetic field flux density, measured time at a different rate and direction of time flow than other timepieces which were outside of the coil's magnetic field influence. The caduceus/tensor coil (with proper frequency/voltage) supposedly creates scalar electromagnetic waves that travel at super-luminal velocities (i.e., faster than light speeds).

"As an electronics engineer, there is one thing that comes to mind regarding this. When an electromagnetic field is created, any thing within the densest portion of that field tends to take on the same potential, polarity, frequency, and velocity of that field. This applies both to life forms and inanimate objects.

"Some people refer to an objects, or life forms, energy as its 'aura,' electromagnetic field, or Kirlian field. In fact, there is a little used, formula known as the 'Johnson Effect' which can be used to ascertain the power levels of an object's, or life form's, electromagnetic

Time Travel – Fact Not Fiction

field. The reason it was discarded is because it leans toward inaccuracy at frequencies above the Earth's magnetic field frequency, which is about 7.8 Hz.

"With respect to what I've mentioned, I believe Einstein's theory of relativity states that if an electromagnetic wave were to (somehow) be propagated at velocities beyond the speed of light, then that wave would move backward in time. Or, more specifically stated, that the Universe's 'time' would start going backward relative to the time experienced by the wave (which, if a wave could have consciousness, would experience a normal, forward, progressive 'time'). I believe this is what happened to my friend when he was operating his machine. By the way, he was wearing a digital watch when this happened (the first time). However, the static charge he experienced blew the digital timer circuitry inside the watch."

Other Time Machines

Steven L. Gibbs (R.R.1, Box 79, Clearwater, NE. 68726) has a time machine. In fact, for $360, Steven Gibbs has a time machine that anyone can buy and try out for themselves. Called the Hyperdimensional Resonator (HDR), Gibbs machine is the result of a strange incident where supposedly his future self sent a letter to his past self.

Gibbs told *Strange* magazine editor Mark Chorvinsky, that back in 1981he found a letter claiming to have been written by his future self. The writer predicted accurately that Gibbs would be soon involved with time travel. Gibbs is not sure if the letter was really from his future self or from an alternate double from an alternate future universe.

Inspired by his unusual message, Gibbs started experimenting with sonic resonators and eventually developed the HDR. His first reported success came in 1985 when Mike Arklinski, author of the book **Time Travel Today**, bought a HDR unit from Gibbs and activated it "over a natural grid point up in Great Falls." Arklinski allegedly went physically back to 1945 and stayed there for six hours. On his second attempt he went back to the year 1895 and stayed there for two hours.

Arklinski told Gibbs that he visited some of the old saloons back in those days. "They were nothing like what they say the old West was in the movies." Gibbs said in *Strange* magazine (issue fourteen, 1994), that when his HDR unit is activated over a large natural grid point, someone could travel physically through time. California is apparently a good place for time travelers because "...there are so

Time Travel – Fact Not Fiction

doggone many grids up in the California area that anybody who activates one of my HDR units in California is pretty much going to travel physically through time whether they like it or not. Except for maybe a few when they might be positioned in a place far from a grid. But in most cases though the people who have bought units from me have been transported. And some of them haven't even gotten back, from what I've heard. And that's kind of the danger involved in physical time travel."

The HDR is described as a two dial, one bank treatment instrument, which plugs into a normal 110V outlet. This device generates an AC/DC, 60-cycle, alternating frequency which generates an unlimited amount of white light energy. It comes equipped with a witness well, phenolic rubbing plate, multidimensional stabilizer, clear switch, power switch, time coils and one electromagnet.

Among other things, the unit allegedly can also be used for out of the body time travel. Each unit has a built-in electronic sensor coil which is directly beneath the rubbing plate. These coils are specifically designed to pick-up and amplify thought induced white energy.

The device works like a Radionics machine. After the unit has been connected to a 110Voutlet, the dials on the machine are then tuned radionically for the year, month and day that you wish to travel to. This is done with the time coils positioned around the head. After the rates have been found, the unit is activated and the electromagnet is placed over the solar plexus for three minutes.

After the treatment is over, the unit is deactivated and the time coils are removed. The person now finds a comfortable place to relax in order for the energies to take effect. If everything has been done correctly, you will then be projected to the year, month and day you selected. This process can take awhile to perfect. Often, the unit will appear not to work, but when the time is checked it will show that several minutes have been either lost or gained. This is a good sign that you are on the right track. Keep trying, it will work.

The Russian Time Machine

Russian scientists are also interested in the mysteries of time and supposedly they have been experimenting with a machine that can physically alter time for anything inside of it. Paul Stonehill, researcher of Russian paranormal events, reports that the time machine the Russians created is currently limited. It can only slow time or speed it up by four minutes in a 24-hour period. Scientists hope that in the

Time Travel – Fact Not Fiction

future the machine will be able to move through Time and Space at much faster speeds. Scientist Vadim Alexandrovich Chernobrov's theory explains time (a physical phenomenon), under certain conditions, as a manifestation of electromagnetic forces. It follows that with the help of such forces time could be influenced. A machine based on such theory can be easily controlled and may be able to provide higher performance.

From 1988 to 1993, four experimental time machines were created. All were lentil shaped machines. They were constructed around a closed space that has special electromagnetic properties. Each also has a control unit, a power unit and instrumentation.

The needed electromagnetic field's configuration is created by a series of electromagnetic operating surfaces nested in each other under the matryoshka principle. (Matryoshkas are the Russian wooden dolls that successively smaller dolls fitted inside them.) These layers of flat electromagnets were twisted into an ellipsoidal shape.

The volume of payload in the center of the machine was about the size of a soccer ball. Therefore, mice were used for the experiments. The first experiments which transported insects and mice into the past, killed the experimental animals, despite the time difference of only two seconds. Those humans who were not careful and stood too close to the time machine during the experiment developed symptoms similar to those reported by sailors who allegedly participated in the Philadelphia Experiment.

After the layout of the machine was improved, the animal test pilots survived the process. In 2011, Chernobrov released further information saying his time machine is a metal sphere and has a diameter of two meters. Inside is housed a meter wide space that can house a time traveling chrononaut. The device achieves travel through time, according to its inventor, by utilizing strong magnetic fields that resonate about the capsule and affect the natural flow of time and causality by literally increasing or slowing the flow of time.

During experiments, Chernobrov has shown that very precise chronometers, synchronized before the field is energized, experience a significant divergence in time after one has been placed inside the time machine while the other is kept far from the energized field as a control. The chronometers revealed time is definitely warped within the machine's magnetic fields.

According to an article translated by Lena Ksandinova, "the first Russian time machine was constructed by the scientists of Moscow Aircraft University. To understand, how the machine impacts live

Time Travel – Fact Not Fiction

creatures, Vadim Chernobrov, an experiment administrator, put cockroaches inside. The insects died. They modernized the machine and put mice inside. The effect on them was the same. Scientists realized what the cause of death was: on different parts of the body time ran with a different speed. They fixed the machine once again and put a puppy called 'Lunar Rover' inside. He was inside for 108 minutes. The puppy survived, but behaved like he was having rabies.

"Then experiments on people came. Nine scientists, among which was Chernobrov, took part in it. Instruments inside the machine recorded a 3-percent time shift, and changes in machine size. Experiment participants, however, felt nothing but moderate arrhythmia and colored circles in eyes."

The experiment with people was the most dangerous. Some scientists familiar with the experiment condemned it as reckless.

"We came to conclusion that time is 3–dimensional," explained Chernobrov. "So in fact we can move in time backwards and forwards."

As Ksandinova reported, a larger model of the time machine was built to carry humans. It was constructed in a remote forest in Russia's Volgograd Region. While the device had a low power capacity it still affected the flow of time by three per cent; that temporal permutation was measured with symmetrical crystal oscillators. At first, the researchers spent periods of five, ten and later, twenty minutes in the field of the time machine; the longest stay recorded lasted about half an hour. Chernobrov reported the volunteers felt as if they had shifted into a different world: "they felt life here and *there* at the same time as if some space was unfolding."

Chernobrov believes that humans will be able to travel through time in the 21st century. According to preliminary data, time has many measures: it is heterogeneous and changeable. The present is but a passage of the multivaried future into the monovaried past. Travel into the future is possible only through one branch, but the return to the present is possible through any of the branches, because they will all return the time machine to the primordial point.

Travel into the past guarantees that the time machine will come to any event that has occurred. And if the visit does not result in undesirable contacts and the movement of history is not altered, the return to the starting line should not be hindered. Otherwise, the return will take place through another branch. But the movement of history will change only for the time travelers: They will not be able to get to the point from which they started and will find themselves in another version of the present – that is, in a parallel world. This eliminates any paradoxes, such as the old brain teaser of going back and murdering ones grandfather.

Professor Ronald Mallett's Time Machine

University of Connecticut physics professor Ronald Mallett is convinced that time travel will become a reality sooner rather than later. "What I'm doing, I like to think of as analogous to the Wright brothers," he says. "They sent this rickety craft across a few hundred yards of beach. But with the technological acceleration that happened after that, by the middle of the century we had intercontinental air travel. This is only the beginning. Once it can be shown to be done, even in the simplest case, then what we learn from that will be incredible."

Einstein showed that mass and energy are the same thing. The time machine, as conceived by Prof. Mallett, uses light in the form of circulating lasers to warp or loop time instead of using massive objects.

Prof. Mallett's theoretical research shows that light and not just matter could affect gravity. Mallett has proposed creating a machine which circulates laser beams to create space-time dragging for an elementary particle. Creating a ring of light, in a cyclotron-like machine will create a gravitational drag effect, this will be noticeable for small elementary particles, such as a neutron. However the machine will not have an effect on any other matter outside of the apparatus itself. The function of time-dragging will operate within the local reference frame of the matter trapped within a cyclotron stream. This does not make a time machine for an external observer, but will create time dilation effect on matter caught in the light-stream's drag.

In other words, at sufficient energies, the circulating laser might produce not just frame-dragging but also closed time-like curves, allowing time travel into the past. For the strong gravitational field of a circulating cylinder of light, Prof. Mallett says that he has found new exact solutions of the Einstein field equations for the exterior and interior gravitational fields of the light cylinder. The exterior gravitational field is shown to contain closed time-like lines. The presence of closed time-like lines indicates the possibility of time travel into the past. This creates the foundation for a time machine based on a circulating cylinder of light.

"Say you have a cup of coffee and a spoon," Mallett explained. "The coffee is empty space, and the spoon is the circulating light beam. When you stir the coffee with the spoon, the coffee – or the empty space – gets twisted. Suppose you drop a sugar cube in the coffee. If empty space were twisting, you'd be able to detect it by observing a subatomic particle moving around in the space." And according to Einstein, whenever you do something to space, you also affect time. Twisting space causes time to be twisted, meaning you could theoretically walk through time as you walk through space.

To determine if time loops exist, Mallett has designed a desktop-sized device that will test his time-warping theory. By arranging mirrors, Mallett can make a circulating light beam which should warp surrounding space. Because some subatomic particles have extremely short lifetimes, Mallett hopes that he will observe these particles to exist for a longer time than expected when placed in the vicinity of the circulating light beam. A longer lifetime means that the particles must have flowed through a time loop into the future.

Recently, Prof. Mallett, in a rare collaboration between theoretical and experimental physicists, has been working with his UConn physics colleague Chandra Roychoudhuri, a research professor who specializes in lasers, on the prototype.

"Not only do you want high-intensity laser beams, but over a very small region," he explains. "The effect becomes greater the smaller the area."

If that experiment succeeds, then it would be on to the next: trying to confirm that that twisting of space leads to the twisting of time. The idea is to drop tiny neutrons into that tortioned space. If Mallett's theories held water, the subatomic particles would travel fractions of a second backward in time.

Some people show concern over time traveling, although Mallett, an advocate of the Parallel Universes theory, assures us that time machines will not present any danger. "The Grandfather Paradox (where you go back in time and kill your grandfather) is not an issue," said Mallett. "In a sense, time travel means that you're traveling both in time and into other universes. If you go back into the past, you'll go into another universe. As soon as you arrive at the past, you're making a choice and there'll be a split. Our universe will not be affected by what you do in your visit to the past."

Funding for his program, now known as The Space-time Twisting by Light (STL) project, is progressing. Nevertheless, when the Defense Advanced Research Projects Agency, a branch of the United States Defense Department, offered much needed funding, Mallett turned them down.

"I'm trying to avoid military funding," he said. "They could, at some point, slap top-secret on me and take the project away."

Time Travel – Fact Not Fiction

Scientist Receives Public Funding for Time Travel Research

A University of Washington scientist who could not obtain funding from traditional research agencies to test his idea that light particles act in reverse time has received more than $35,000 from people nationwide who didn't want to see this admittedly far-fetched idea go unexplored.

"This country puts a lot more money into things that seem to me much crazier than this," said Mitch Rudman, a music industry executive in Las Vegas whose family foundation donated $20,000 to the experiment. "It's outrageous to me that talented scientists have to go looking for a few bucks to do anything slightly outside the box."

What John Cramer is proposing to do is certainly outside the box. It's about quantum retrocausality.

"He's looking into the fundamental qualities of the universe," said Denny Gmur, a scientist who works for a biotechnology firm in Bothell. "I had $2,000 set aside to buy myself a really nice guitar, but I thought, you know, I'd rather support something that's really mind-boggling and cool."

Cramer, a physicist, for decades has been interested in resolving a fundamental paradox of quantum mechanics, the theory that accounts for the behavior of matter and energy at subatomic levels. It's called the Einstein-Podolsky-Rosen paradox.

It was set up by Albert Einstein (and two other guys named Rosen and Podolsky) in the 1930s to try to prove the absurdity of quantum theory. Einstein didn't like quantum theory, especially one aspect of it he ridiculed as "spooky action at a distance" because it seemed to require subatomic particles interacting faster than the speed of light.

However, experimental evidence has continued to pile up demonstrating the spooky action. Two subatomic particles split from a single particle do somehow instantaneously communicate no matter how far apart they get in space and time. The phenomenon is described as "entanglement" and "non-local communication."

For example, one high-energy photon split by a prism into two lower-energy photons could travel into space and separate by many light years. If one of the photons is somehow forced up, the other photon – even if impossibly distant – will instantly tilt down to compensate and balance out both trajectories.

As the evidence for this has accumulated, several fairly contorted and unsatisfying efforts have been aimed at solving the puzzle. Cramer has proposed an explanation that doesn't violate the speed of light but

Time Travel – Fact Not Fiction

does kind of mess with the traditional concept of time. As weird as it may seem, Cramer suggests that it could involve signaling, or communication, in reverse time. Physicists John Wheeler and Richard Feynman years ago promoted this idea of retrocausality as worth considering. Cramer's version aimed at using retrocausality to resolve the EPR paradox is dubbed (by him) the "transactional interpretation of quantum mechanics."

Most physicists, such as the celebrated cosmologist Stephen Hawking, still believe time can move only in one direction – forward. Cramer contends there is no hard and fast reason why.

He has proposed a relatively simple bench-top experiment using lasers, prisms, splitters, fiber-optic cables and other gizmos to first see if he can detect "non-local" signaling between entangled photons. He hopes to get it going in July. If this succeeds, he hopes to get support from "traditional funding sources" to really scale up and test for photons communicating in reverse time.

"I'm not crazy," he confirmed. "I don't know if this experiment will work, but I can't see why it won't. People are skeptical about this, but I think we can learn something, even if it fails."

Not too long ago, Cramer thought he would not even be allowed to fail. None of the standard scientific funding agencies wanted any part of the project. NASA's Institute for Advanced Concepts sent Cramer a rejection letter, adding it was getting out of the advanced concepts business anyway – now that most of the space agency's money is going to the federal government's renewed push into manned spaceflight.

The most creative branch of the military-science-industrial complex (known as DARPA, Defense Advanced Research Projects Agency) also rejected Cramer's proposal. Officials at DARPA told the UW physicist his experiment is "too weird."

"I thought we were going to have to pull the plug," Cramer said. But when word of his funding plight went out across the Internet a few months ago after a Seattle P-I article, people like Rudman and Gmur began contacting the UW to see if they could lend some support.

"Heck, if it works we can go back in time and get our money back," laughed John Crow, a businessman who splits his time between his gas-and-oil business in Shreveport and a home in Port Angeles. Crow donated $3,000 because he found Cramer's approach too fascinating not to try. He said that he was a "crass businessman, but in business we know high risk offers high reward. This isn't that much money to find out if time can go both forward and backward."

Time Travel – Fact Not Fiction

Walter Kistler, a retired physicist and rocket scientist who started Redmond-based Kistler Aerospace, donated $5,000. Kistler's company struggled for many years unsuccessfully promoting the concept of reusable rockets, even going bankrupt once, but recently won a NASA contract.

"I know how difficult it can be to get people to even consider new or unusual ideas," he said. "Even Einstein had trouble accepting the basic ideas of quantum theory. I've talked to professor Cramer, and what he is trying to do could be very important."

Kistler said he was overjoyed to hear that other people thought this was worth supporting.

"Artists have experienced non-local space all along, we just can't prove it," said Richard Miller, an artist and photographer in Port Townsend. Miller, who prefers not to disclose the amount of his donation, said he's not worried about the strong possibility of failure here.

"I would say the predicted failure of this project is probably a good omen," he said. "Most predictions are wrong."

Cramer said it's possible that the primary goal of his experiment could fail and yet still produce something of value. Some new subtlety about the nature of entanglement could be revealed, he said, even if the photons don't engage in measurable non-local communication. The "disentanglement" itself, he said, could be quite revealing.

"It wouldn't be as nice as a positive result, but it would certainly be interesting and publishable," Cramer said. If there is an interesting negative result or a half-positive result, he said he will buy more precise equipment to see if he can tease out what's happening. Cramer has all the money he needs for this phase, but he hopes to see a second phase.

In the music business, said Rudman, the Las Vegas music mogul, most records they produce don't do well. In the vernacular, he said, "They stiff."

"But the rare hits we get every once in a while pay for all the stiffs, and then some," Rudman said. "If this stiffs, it stiffs. But, man, you've got to try, don't you? You've got to be willing to take the risk of being wrong to find something new."

Just in case you were wondering why DARPA refused to fund Cramer's research, it may be because they were working on something equally as bizarre as they recently came out and admitted that they have had some success in their own time-related experiments.

Time Travel – Fact Not Fiction

American scientists working for the Pentagon have published research which demonstrates how to hide history as it happens. A team at Cornell University working with the Defense Advanced Research Projects Agency (Darpa) has published a report in the journal Nature demonstrating how to hide an event for 40 trillionths of a second.

The effect, described as "spatio-temporal cloaking," depends on the ability to slow the flow of light from events as they occur - making them impossible to observe. Researchers passed a beam of green light through a lens while travelling inside a fiber-optic cable. The lens split the light into one slow beam and one fast beam, and then fired a red laser into the same space. The red laser was not visible, because it was fired during the gap between the different green lasers.

To achieve spatial cloaking, the index of refraction is manipulated to flow light from a probe around an object in such a way that a 'hole' in space is created, and the object remains hidden. Alternatively, it may be desirable to cloak the occurrence of an event over a finite time period, and the idea of temporal cloaking has been proposed in which the dispersion of the material is manipulated in time, producing a 'time hole' in the probe beam to hide the occurrence of the event from the observer.

Lawyer Claims To Have Participated in Time Travel Project

Does the United State have top secret teleportation and time travel technology? The answer is yes, according to Andrew D. Basiago, a lawyer from the state of Washington. Basiago says that from the time he was seven-years-old to when he was 12, he participated in *Project Pegasus*, a secret program that developed teleportation and time travel under the Defense Advanced Research Projects Agency (DARPA).

Even though it may sound strange that children were possibly used in these early time travel experiments, similar claims had been made by Al Bielak, Preston Nichols, Stewart Swerdlow, Duncan O'Finioan and others, especially with the Montauk time travel project. Early experiments allegedly used orphans from South America, and many did not survive the rigors of theses early tests. Basiago says that he got involved in Project Pegasus through his father who was an engineer for the project. Accordingly, DARPA had five reasons for involving American school children in such new, dangerous, and experimental activities.

1. The Department of Defense wanted to test the mental and physical effects of teleportation on children.

Time Travel – Fact Not Fiction

2. Project Pegasus needed to use children because the holograms created by the chronovisors would collapse when adults stood within them.

3. The children were tabula rasa and would tend to see things during the time probes that adults would tend to miss.

4. The children were trainees who upon growing up would serve in a covert time-space program under DARPA that would operate in tandem with the overt space program under NASA.

5. The program sponsors found that after moving between time lines, adult time travelers were often becoming insane, and it was hoped that by working with gifted and talented children from childhood, the US government might create an adult cadre of "chrononauts" capable of dealing with the psychological effects of time travel.

Basiago said he experienced eight different time travel technologies during his stint in the program. Mostly, he said, his travel involved a teleporter based on technical papers found in Nikola Tesla's New York City apartment after his death in January 1943. Scientists were shocked when they realized that Tesla had discovered the science behind teleportation, even though the technology to make Tesla's idea workable was not available while he was alive.

"The machine consisted of two gray elliptical booms about eight feet tall, separated by about 10 feet, between which a shimmering curtain of what Tesla called 'radiant energy' was broadcast," Basiago said. ""Radiant energy is a form of energy that Tesla discovered that is latent and pervasive in the universe and has among its properties the capacity to bend time and space."

Basiago said project participants would jump through this field of radiant energy into a vortal tunnel and "when the tunnel closed, we found ourselves at our destination. One felt either as if one was moving at a great rate of speed or moving not at all, as the universe was wrapped around one's location."

The Tesla-Based teleportation machinery was fully operational by 1967-68, but what was even more amazing is that not only could this technology teleport through space, it was also capable of teleportation through time.

Basiago claims that through this time travel technology, he can be seen in a photograph at Gettysburg in 1863, which he said he visited in 1972 via a plasma confinement chamber located in East Hanover, N.J. Unfortunately, the trip ripped his shoes and socks off of his feet.

Time Travel – Fact Not Fiction

"I had been dressed in period clothing, as a Union bugle boy," he said. "I attracted so much attention at the Lincoln speech site at Gettysburg – wearing over-sized men's street shoes – that I left the area around the dais and walked about 100 paces over to where I was photographed in the Josephine Cogg image of Lincoln at Gettysburg."

In addition, Basiago said he traveled to Ford's Theatre the night of Lincoln's assassination on five or six occasions. "I did not, however, witness the assassination," he said. "Once, I was on the theater level when he was shot and I heard the shot followed by a great commotion that arose from the crowd. It was terrible to hear."

Basiago said each of his visits to the past was different, "like they were sending us to slightly different alternative realities on adjacent timelines. As these visits began to accumulate, I twice ran into myself during two different visits."

Being sent back in time to the same place and moment, but from different starting points in the present, allowed two of himselves to be in Ford's Theatre at the same time in 1865.

"After the first of these two encounters with myself occurred, I was concerned that my cover might be blown," he recalled. "Unlike the jump to Gettysburg, in which I was clutching a letter to Navy Secretary Gideon Welles to offer me aid and assistance in the event I was arrested, I didn't have any explanatory materials when I was sent to Ford's Theatre."

And how did these alleged time travelers return to the present day or their point of origin? According to Basiago, some sort of holographic technology allowed them to travel both physically and virtually.

"If we were in the hologram for 15 minutes or fewer," he explained, "the hologram would collapse, and after about 60 seconds of standing in a field of super-charged particles...we would find ourselves back on the stage...in the present."

Basiago said the technology should only be used for real-time teleportation, not time travel, because, "It would be chaos."

Between 1969 and 1972, as a child participant in Project Pegasus, Basiago says that he viewed past and future events through a device known as a chronovisor. The chronovisor was created in the 1950s by a Benedictine monk named Father Pellegrino Ernetti. Father Ernetti was a specialist on archaic music, such as Georgoian chants, and wondered if there was a way to capture and view the energy that still existed from the past. The chronovisor was described as a large cabinet with a cathode ray tube for viewing the received events and a series of buttons, levers, and other controls for selecting the time and the location to be viewed. It could also focus and track specific people. According to its inventor, it worked by receiving, decoding and reproducing the electromagnetic radiation left behind from past events, though it could also pick up sound waves.

His training, Basiago said, culminated in 1981, when, as a 19-year-old, he teleported to Mars, first by himself after being prepared for the trip by CIA officer Courtney M. Hunt, and then a second time in the company of Hunt. Both trips, Basiago said, were made via a "jump room" located at a CIA facility at 999 North Sepulveda Boulevard, El Segundo, California just south of and across the street from the Los Angeles International Airport. The apparent purpose of the trips to Mars was to familiarize him with Mars because the CIA knew of his destiny pertaining to publicly establishing the fact that Mars is an inhabited planet and deemed it important that he visit Mars and experience its conditions first-hand.

During one time probe to the future, Basiago viewed the U.S. Supreme Court building in Washington, DC as it would be in the year 2013. During this probe, he found that the Supreme Court building was under 100 feet of stagnant water and reported this to the Lieutenant Commander from the Office of Naval Intelligence who debriefed him after the probe to the future was completed. He hastens to add that because the chronovisors did not identify absolute, deterministic futures but rather alternate futures in the "multi-verse," this catastrophic vision of Washington, DC might be from an alternative time line that does not materialize on our time line.

In contrast to the chronovisor probes, in which a form of virtual time travel was achieved, the teleporters developed by Project Pegasus allowed for physical teleportation to distant locations, sometimes with an adjustment forward or backward in time of days, weeks, months, or years. According to Basiago, by 1972, the U.S. government was using "quantum displacement" of this kind to both send people forward in time several years to store sensitive military secrets in the future and backward in time several years to provide the government current intelligence about future events.

So what has happened to this amazing technology in the years after Basiago's participation? He says he is not certain, and wonders why it still continues to be highly compartmentalized and top secret. Basiago thinks that such amazing technology should be used for the benefit of all, and would certainly help solve a lot of the problems facing mankind today.

Time Travel – Fact Not Fiction

"Imagine a world in which one could jump through Grand Central Teleport in New York City, travel through a tunnel in the time-space continuum, and emerge several seconds later at Union Teleport in Los Angeles. Such a world has been possible since 1967-68, when teleportation was first achieved by DARPA's Project Pegasus, only to be suppressed ever since as a secret weapon. When my quest, Project Pegasus, succeeds, such a world will emerge, and human beings linked by teleportation around the globe will proclaim that the Time-Space Age has begun."

Die Glocke – A Nazi Time Machine?

The Nazi Bell (Die Glocke) was first brought to the public's attention from the book *The Search for Zero Point*, by Nick Cook. The Germans were working on a number of secret projects during WWII in search of a "Wunderwaffe," or Wonder Weapon, something that would stop the Allies advance once and for all. Allegedly, the Nazi Bell was a device to test anti-gravity theories and was more-than-likely part of Nazi Germany's secret atomic weapons project. What is known about the bell is that it was a centrifuge device shaped like a bell with a hemispherical domed top. The outer bell was made of three inch thick ceramic, much like a high voltage porcelain insulator.

From its description, the bell sounds like a heavy particle accelerator, used as an artificial neutron source to breed Protactinium 233 from Thorium 232. Protactinium would naturally degrade after 27 days into pure bomb grade Uranium 233. Uranium 233 derived from spent reactor waste is often contaminated by Uranium 232 when Thorium 230 gets bombarded by a second neutron, but in a particle accelerator this process does not have time to occur and thus U232 contamination is as low as one part per million and thus as safe to handle as weapons grade Plutonium.

Inside the bell was located two contra rotating drums. Norwegian born physicist Rolf Wideroe wrote in his autobiography about development of the bell at Hamburg, by the company CHF Muller. In his patent his diagrams showed one sphere inside another spun on a common axle. As is common with particle accelerators a vacuum has to be created to propagate plasma inside these evacuated chambers. Then heated mercury vapour would have been bled into the cavity and then once spun up subjected to powerful discharges of electricity to ionise the Mercury. Under this influence the Mercury would fluoresce and photons would collide with extremely energetic electrons, creating Gamma X-rays. These X-rays in turn would stimulate the Beryllium oxide in the Xerum 525 to emit thermal neutrons. In turn these thermal neutrons would be absorbed by the Thorium 232 changing it into Protactinium 233.

The Nazi Bell was initially housed in a basement beneath the Charity hospital in Berlin and thus the project was known as Charite Anlage. From November 1943 the Nazi bell was housed in an underground laboratory beneath Gandau airfield on the western outskirts of Breslau, now known as the Polish city of Wroclaw. Xerum 525 compounds were supplied from a laboratory in the city of Danzig now known as Gydina. After operation the spent and altered compound was reprocessed at a laboratory west of Breslau then known as Neuberg.

It was shifted from Gandau in November 1944 to Furstenstein Castle and later in December 1944 located inside Wenceslas mine. Following the war Professor Manfred von Ardenne led two Soviet scientists Nicolai Flyerov (aka N.I. Frolov) and Igor Kurchatov to the Wenceslas mine and gave them a description of installing what he called a cyclotron in the mine. This mine was abandoned before the war. Above ground there was a power station with two steam cooling towers. The bases of these have become known by various names like the "Henge" after Stonehenge, or the Fly Trap.

John Dering – a physicist specializing advanced directed energy, nonlinear electrodynamics, and new energy sources – has further reported on a "Rhine Valley" facility and device. He believes this to have been an actual wartime prototype deployment of a successor to the Nazi Bell experiments, which were carried out in the Wenceslas Mine research lab in occupied Poland. While the Bell experiment was focused on developing a radical new propulsion technology, the little-known Rhine Valley experiment may have been a last-ditch attempt to weaponize the Bell's dangerous side effect for use against Allied forces.

Dering speculates that the German WWII research was intended to create a powerful propulsion effect by engineering application of Einstein's Unified Field Theory (UFT) equations. Within the 1929 version of the Einstein UFT equations, a linkage is found between the "Vector Magnetic Potential" and Torsion. Put simply, in the Unified Field Theory, the effects of curved space-time (resulting from a massive body, like the Earth) can locally offset by creating Torsion. Thus electromagnetic interactions are harnessed to induce torsion, which in turn can then null out gravitation. This astounding possibility for gravity control is not predicted in either the Special or General Relativity theories and appears only in the Unified Field equations. Thus, a sort of counteraction to gravity or "anti-gravity" field would be the result.

Time Travel – Fact Not Fiction

It's not known where the true inspiration for the Nazi Bell device and prior Rhine-Valley experiments originated. But it's possible to speculate that they were trying to leap to a completely electromagnetic propulsion system after realizing the limited potential in controllability and speed from their experimentation with the Coanda-Effect saucer technology. Perhaps some of the more forward-thinking physicists had the ear of Hans Kammler and suggested to him that the time was right to evolve to a technology so far ahead of aerodynamic propulsion of the day that it would give Germany absolute supremacy in the air. Darker possibilities exist, given that the Bell Device researchers appeared very interested in the dangerous and lethal side effects created by exposure to the Bell force field.

Assuming that the Nazi's had decided on a nearly fictional approach to directly interacting with gravity through electromagnetism, the next logical step that they would have taken is to find a scientific basis to work from. As scientists, Kammler's team would have quickly realized that this scientific support wouldn't have come from either Relativity Theory or Quantum Mechanics. But they wouldn't have had to search very far as the Germans had already reviewed just such a theory to unify Electromagnetism and Gravitational Forces.

On June 14, 1928, a paper was published in German that would have certainly attracted the attention of anyone looking for a quick and easy way to convert from electricity to gravitational force. The English translation of the title is "New possibility for a Unified Field Theory of Gravitation and Electricity". It contains the beginnings of what later became known as Torsion Theory. Despite the Nazi dislike for Jewish science and culture, this paper was written by a physicist too renowned to be ignored. Quite possibly the World's greatest physicist, Albert Einstein.

Starting in the early 1920s, Einstein and others began to speculate that General Relativity (which describes gravitation and space-time) could be modified to include the laws of Maxwell that describe electromagnetism. In essence, Einstein sought to show that the laws of electricity and magnetism could be "unified" with the laws of gravitation. In other words, such a theory would imply that all electrical and magnetic effects and all gravity effects are manifestations of an underlying "Unified Field". By the late 1920s, Einstein's papers on Unified Field theory began to be read by physicists interested in exploring experimental verification of his theories.

John Dering has suggested that in addition to a general familiarity with Einstein's Unified Field Theory from written publications, the Nazi's may have in fact had "inside information" on the subject. Supposedly,

Time Travel – Fact Not Fiction

Gerlach had discussed the foundations of this new Unified Field Theory at length with Einstein while the theory was being formulated, and had also collaborated with Einstein during the 1920s on a search for experimental verification. As History tells us, Gerlach was later appointed to the position of "plenipotentiary" for Nazi Fission Research in 1944 by the Reich Research Council giving him top-level scientific connections throughout Germany's cutting-edge research programs. Nick Cook has also highlighted Gerlach's connection to the Nazi-Bell project through the testimony of defense journalist Igor Witkowski, who claims to have been shown documents identifying Gerlach's involvement in the project.

Thus, with the driving goal of building an electromagnetically-powered UFO to replace the less-than-spectacular performance of the Coanda-Effect flying disks, Kammler's scientific team would have already been familiar with Einstein's work in gravity and would have had a real basis from the published UFT tensor equations to begin rapid experimentation with a new technology for 1940's era anti-gravity.

The other interesting aspect about the Nazi Bell has to do with the fact that if you generate a torsion field of sufficient magnitude the theory says you can bend the four dimensions of space around the generator. In other words, when you bend space, you also bend time. If that is the case, were the Nazi's working on an anti-gravity device and by accident discovered a time machine? We may never know.

Tesla Time Travel Experiments
By Commander X

I have long been an admirer of the great inventor Nikola Tesla. That should come to no surprise to anyone who has read some of my previous books. Here was a man whose genius was far beyond the great minds of his day. He had an intellect that at times seemed almost unearthly. I suppose this is why some have speculated that such a remarkable individual could not have sprung from the bosom of mother Earth, but instead was the product of extraterrestrial intervention.

I must admit that for a while the idea that Nikola Tesla was not of this planet held a certain appeal to me. It would certainly answer a lot of questions about this enigmatic man - but of course it would also create even more questions that would be impossible to answer in my lifetime. So I was finally left with the simplest explanation on the true origins of Nikola Tesla. I have concluded he was an extraordinary human the likes we so rarely see.

Time Travel – Fact Not Fiction

My primary schooling was bereft of any education of Tesla or his great achievements. His name, in its absence, spoke of dark conspiracies and downright thievery. In public, only the Tesla-coil stands out in honor of its namesake, but few know of the person for whom it is christened. Textbooks held no place between its pages for this great man, and teachers rarely uttered his name. Thankfully, some have come to recognize the great injustice that has been done to Tesla and have found a place in some classrooms to teach his history. I think it would be safe to say that Nikola Tesla was the man who invented the 20th Century.

But a mystery remains.

A mystery that has been diabolical in its treachery not only to Nikola Tesla, but to humanity as a whole.

We know that the United State Patent Office granted patents to many of Tesla's inventions. These were inventions that Tesla and his investors saw as potentially profitable – the AC motor is an excellent example of one of Tesla's inventions that changed the world. However, Tesla also invented an unknown number of other items that were never patented for one reason or another. Tesla had a keen sense of what would garner financial interest, but he also worked on and developed technology that was simply for his own curiosity. Of these inventions, we know practically nothing.

Remarkable by any standard, Tesla's patents illuminate only his most purposive, practical work. As he often lamented, there just wasn't enough time to tame the racing of ideas in his head; so much had to be left incomplete. Some of the projects, achieving an ultrahigh vacuum, a rocket engine design, experiments in directed beams and solar power, simply don't fit into the early 20th Century. Frequently he was content to publish his findings without regard to priority or patentability: he introduced in this way the therapeutic method now called diathermy. Other ideas were simply written down with no attempt to patent or even publicize them.

We now know that Tesla was interested and experimented in such "wild" ideas as free energy, antigravity, invisibility and even time travel. It's no surprise that Tesla in his day was loathe to speak of these kinds of interests – after all, even today these areas of study still come under fire by some "mainstream" scientists, who refuse to use their imaginations and intellect, and scorn such interests with terms such as "bad science" and quackery.

In my years as a military intelligence operative I came into contact with a number of top-secret programs that were either

Time Travel – Fact Not Fiction

investigating, or, shockingly enough, actively using technology based on some of Tesla's "wild" ideas. Both the United States and Russia have active Particle Beam and RF (radio frequency) weaponry that has been in operation since the early 1970's – all as a result of Tesla's early 19th and 20th Century experiments.

To say that there are other black budget projects involving Tesla-based research would wildly underestimate the total amount of research and development being conducted right now by many countries worldwide. And these are the projects that we know about. Who knows how many deep, dark, secret projects are being conducted right now with science that could be decades, even hundreds of years beyond what civilian science knows today.

In 1895, while conducting research with his step-up transformer, Nikola Tesla had his first indications that time and space could be influenced by using highly charged, rotating magnetic fields. Part of this revelation came about from Tesla's experimentation with radio frequencies and the transmission of electrical energy through the atmosphere. Tesla's simple discovery would, years later, lead to the infamous Philadelphia Experiment and the Montauk time travel projects. But even before these highly top-secret military programs came about, Tesla made some fascinating discoveries on the nature of time and the real possibilities of time travel.

With these experiments in high-voltage electricity and magnetic fields, Tesla discovered that time and space could be breached, or warped, creating a "doorway" that could lead to other time frames. But with this monumental discovery, Tesla also discovered, through personal experience, the very real dangers inherent with time travel.

Tesla's first brush with time travel came in March 1895. A reporter for the *New York Herald* wrote on March 13 that he came across the inventor in a small café, looking shaken after being hit by 3.5 million volts, "I am afraid," said Tesla, "that you won't find me a pleasant companion tonight. The fact is I was almost killed today. The spark jumped three feet through the air and struck me here on the right shoulder. If my assistant had not turned off the current instantly in might have been the end of me."

Tesla, on contact with the resonating electromagnetic charge, found himself outside his time-frame reference. He reported that he could see the immediate past – present and future, all at once. But he was paralyzed within the electromagnetic field, unable to help himself. His assistant, by turning off the current, released Tesla before any permanent damage was done. A repeat of this very incident would occur years later during the Philadelphia Experiment. Unfortunately, the sailors involved were   left outside their time-frame reference for too long with disastrous results.

Tesla's secret time travel experiments would continue on in the hands of others who were not as concerned with humanity as Tesla. We are left with rumors and speculations on who may have become the heirs of Tesla's research – hopefully, someday these secrets will be revealed once and for all.

The Wave Rider

Former radio talk show host Art Bell, who professes a fascination with the idea of time travel, received a series of faxes in 1998 from someone claiming to be a time traveler and associated with a secret organization known as The Club.   The time traveler told Bell that in 1983 he enlisted in the United States Army, it was shortly afterwards he was approached by those he refers to as My Friends. This group had chosen the time traveler because of certain natural conditions in his physical make-up that made him an excellent candidate to join The Club, a secret group of time travelers.

Called "wave riding," the process of traveling through time involves targeting a particular person, place or event. The more information on the target the better the chance of success. The wave rider takes a photo of the target, a sheet of paper with the information written on it, a map of the site etc. The target is circled and the process is begun. A quiet, darkened area is used for a period of concentration and meditation. The wave rider will study the target for days, weeks, sometimes even months and will eventually begin to dress in the period clothing of the target.

The time traveler then begins to feel the wave approaching and looks for the doorway, gateway, the rip in the fabric of time. The wave rider says that the gateway looks like a pool of water that he passes through before entering the new time line. Some time travelers can only achieve out-of-body type experiences (they are called Projectors). Other, called wave riders, physically disappear from the current time line. The wave rider said that at first he would use a small electromagnetic tuner to help concentrate and focus on the target.

"I was sent back in time on sixteen official missions," reports the wave rider. "I also traveled back on two not-so-official occasions for certain very powerful men. I have also traveled back many times on my own, this is what really got me into trouble. It is unbelievably difficult to create the feared time paradox. On my second mission we tried to create the paradox. We could not. Time is like a river, ever flowing and changing, but always moving forward."

The wave rider told Art Bell that while on a mission to 1999 he discovered that The Club was affiliated with the infamous MJ-12 group, allegedly formed in the 1950s to deal with the UFO problem. The Club is international and many of the more powerful members are actually members of the industrial wealth of Europe and Asia. Their agenda involves using gifted humans to travel the time stream and manipulate people and events for their own hidden purposes. The wave rider is now a fugitive in time and must keep on the move in order to avoid being caught by fellow wave riders sent back to shut him up for good.

Because of the influence of science fiction, time machines have been thought of as the only way to effectively travel in time. However, the technology is still in its infancy. If the wave rider's story is true, then this confirms my suspicion that time travel can be achieved by the power of the human mind. Under the right conditions, some people can move themselves both spiritually and physically across the time stream. There are several different methods which we will examine in the next chapter.

Time Travel – Fact Not Fiction

Original Caption: "Nikola Tesla holding in his hands balls of flame."
Tesla's accident in 1895 may have led to his later Dynamic Theory of
Gravity in which gravity is described as a "field effect." The presence
of highly charged, rotating magnetic fields could therefore influence
time/space within a localized area.

Chapter Eight
Minds Through Time and Space

To the astral body time has no meaning. For many, the ability to project the non-physical self out of the body is as natural as breathing or walking. Out-of-body experiences, also known as Astral Projection or OBEs, are journeys into the astral plane. These journeys can be to the normal, physical world around us, or to the higher levels of reality and even into the past or future. OBEs are one of the more reliable ways to effectively travel through time.

Astral projection can be done by anyone, regardless of age, sex, weight, height. There is, however, one case in which projection should not be practiced, and that is if the projector has heart problems. Astral projection is a breathtaking experience which promises many pleasant surprises. However, any surprise, pleasant or not, will have a dangerous effect on someone with heart problems or weak heart conditions.

The ability to time travel is an important part of our nature. It is something we are all called upon to learn, sooner or later. In order to travel in time we need to know the rules of time. Once these rules are mastered, time can no longer imprison us.

Time travel gives the traveler unbelievable powers of perception and understanding. It is possible to experience a heightening of senses that would amaze the average person. Astral time travel will take you on an incredible journey where you can play cosmic detective in your quest to unravel the mysteries of the ages. Your journey can take you from the farthest reaches of the universe to the unfathomable depths of inner space.

Although astral time travelers usually travel in groups, (as we tend to reincarnate in groups), they belong to no particular race or country. You cannot look at a person who has not yet returned from the future, and tell if they are a potential traveler (to this time period) or not. However, when they do return, they will begin to act differently. Travelers are not always "natural" self-starters. Most require a period of learning. Travel into the past is absolutely necessary

Time Travel – Fact Not Fiction

because it leads to certain essential realizations that can eventually free one from the limitations of Time and Space, and help the rediscovery of unimaginably wonderful states of being. This is a natural and essential part of the phenomenon of human metamorphosis.

The astral time traveler, through the natural progression of their Soul, can experience a vast array of possible futures, over many life times. At some point, an astounding realization is made by the Soul, that all futures are degenerative. (Usually a point where there are no more viable futures . . .) That the primary lesson learned by experiencing the future is, that the act of it somehow violates a fundamental law of balance. The astral time traveler must always realize that the future is an infinite number of possibilities, some are just more probable then others.

Although it was necessary for us to experience the future, to create a structure in time, the act of doing so, has taken us far from our actual natural center in time, and has caused us to experience all manner of unseemly realities. It is at this moment of realization that your Soul gladly lets go of the illusion of future/past, and gravitates automatically, to a balanced point in "Transcended Present Time."

Send Your Astral Body Across The Stream Of Time

Before you try to project your nonphysical self out of the body, you should first have an idea pinpointed in your mind on what you hope to achieve that night. This is called an affirmation. The idea behind affirmations is to implant an intent in your mind before you fall asleep so that you don't neglect your desire to have an OBE when you sleep. Your mind will soon act automatically to induce OBEs.

Our mind easily lets things go when you begin to dream things like worries, ideas, thoughts, all seem to just get lost in a mess of strange imagery. By chanting one of the following affirmations or one of your own, you can increase the chance of keeping your intentions with you.

"I am going to have an out-of-body experience. I am going to let myself drop off to sleep, but I am going to bring this waking consciousness with me wherever I go. I am going to leave my body with full awareness.

"I will travel the astral plane tonight, going as far from my physical body as I so choose, and returning whenever I want, with complete recollection of the experience. Tonight I will travel out-of-body. I am going to allow myself to fall asleep, but I will bring this waking consciousness with me wherever I go. I will leave with full awareness, and recall all that occurs, upon awakening. I will travel safely and my experience will be positive."

Now that you have "programmed" your mind to start the OBE process, you can now use a favorite technique to induce the OBE. Before you do anything, you must first be sure you have no fear of OBEs. You must also be passive, relaxed and patient. There have been hundreds of books written about how to have an OBE and the methods to accomplish this. Listed below are a few techniques that have proved to be the easiest to master for the beginner.

The Floating Technique

Close your eyes and perform your favorite relaxation exercise. Try to imagine that you are underwater and your body is not moving. If you were really underwater in a swimming pool or an ocean, then you should feel your body slowly begin to rise toward the surface. Try to think about what the floating sensation would feel like, and try to re-create it in your mind.

Do not visualize anything, but rather try to "feel" the underwater floating sensation. Keep at this thought and eventually you will leave your body.

The Dropping Technique

Relax in a bed or reclining chair. Take deep breaths, allowing your breath to slow naturally. Do not force it to slow. Induce sensations of "dropping" rapidly through the bed, several inches at a time. These must be quick drops, not slow sinking feelings.

Continue until you feel yourself "on the floor" and then rise again. Allow yourself to drift toward sleep, pulling yourself back each time. Do not physically move your body. Any physical movements could result in the loss of mental control. You should by now be feeling very heavy. As you drift toward sleep, you will see images. Use these images or create your own images to focus on and stay aware.

Soon you will feel vibrations. These are mild and you must remain passive. Visualize yourself floating above your body and feeling the drops. As soon as you have left your body, you will feel a sensation of rushing air, followed by a temporary "blindness" and lightweight feeling. This will take practice, so give it time. Remember, once you are out, move far away from your body or you may be pulled back in. When you want to return, simply visualize your body where you left it. See your house, your room and your body. As soon as you think of this, you will find you are reconnected with your body.

Creative Viewing

The creative viewing method is very simple, but may take several tries before anything happens. It works by guiding you to the awake/asleep line without actually crossing it – an essential step for reaching an experience beyond the physical.

Begin by taking an object that you can focus on and placing it so that you can look at it as you drift off to sleep. You can also try taping a picture to the ceiling and using that, but you want it to be at a comfortable distance so that it doesn't strain your eyes.

Good objects would be unlit candles, small statuettes, stuffed animals, a small mirror, a piece of fruit (apple, orange), a flower, a book, etc. Anything that keeps your interest. If you have a small fish in a fish bowl, you may want to use that. Also, blue or violet toned objects will work best because you will practice in low lighting, and reds can't be seen well in low lights (the human eye can see blues in the dark while reds disappear).

Get comfortable and orient yourself so that you are relaxed, preferably laying or half laying down. Wear loose, comfy clothes. Lights should be dim. Stare at the object, you will begin to get sleepy.

Your body will get heavier and lose most feeling. You will feel like sleeping (your first couple of tries you may end up asleep, but don't worry, try again later). The key is to fight off the tiredness. Your eyelids will get heavy and start to close a bit. Keep as awake as you can (without ever physically moving your body). Your eyes will eventually close but you will still be mentally "looking" at the object.

You will see it and it should seem almost as if you are looking through your eyelids. At this point, your astral and your physical are slightly parted. Imagine slowly floating upward or rolling to the side (without physically doing it). Don't be alarmed when you separate completely. You should be able to look at your physical body from outside it. Congratulations, you are out-of-body.

Remember that the more you try this and the most vigilant you are to staying on the awake side of the w/s (wake/sleep) line the sooner you will have a successful OBE with this method. If you have mastered lucid dreaming, you can easily use this ability to make astral

Time Travel – Fact Not Fiction

traveling easier and more natural for you.   Before sleeping, give yourself a suggestion. Clear the mind, then think something like "I will walk from the dream realm to the astral, and then into the past/future." Then focus on that suggestion as you drift into sleep.   Once you become lucid, you can use several methods to go into the astral/OBE. But the easiest one when you are first trying it out is to go to a high place in the dream (a rooftop, cliff, etc.) and jump.   As you fall you will snap into the astral.

Usually, the first place you will be in the nonphysical is your bedroom, looking at your physical body. Keep your first travel brief so you can remember it when you awake immediately. Better your first trip be short and successful than longer and vague or unclear.   You want to awake aware of the fact that it was an OBE and not a lucid dream.

Once you master this method, you can start by giving yourself the suggestion-- then when you become lucid in a dream, you can just focus on your desire to enter the astral realm, and you will be there.

Manuals of astral travel can be found in any bookstore. Most of these books list various methods for leaving the body.   While these techniques may be fine for honing the creative potential of the mind, or for training the symbolic reflexes, most of them have very little to do with any sort of real exploration of the world beyond Time and Space. True time travel with the astral body is to set the very soul on a course through the potentialities of the unknown universe.

Time travel via the astral body is something that should not be attempted by the spiritual novice.   One should not try to induce an OBE unless he is spiritually motivated and equipped to handle the forces of the unknown.   If the astral traveler understands the basic spiritual rules governing his mobile travel, then it may not be dangerous.

Spontaneously, people have been inadvertently making sudden trips across the time barrier for centuries. The processes of obtaining visions of the future (precognition) and recreations of the past (retrocognition) have become recognized as another uncontrollable facet of psychic phenomena.

If energy, like matter, is indestructible, then the impulse and vibration of every word and deed ever uttered or enacted might still be echoing and pulsating on some psychic ether. The same kind of paranormal mental mechanism that enables the emotions of certain individuals to permeate a room or a house and cause their "ghost" to be seen by those later inhabitants who may possess a similar telepathic affinity, may also cause certain emotionally charged scenes of the past to become imprinted upon the psychic ether and reactivated by those individuals with the proper attunement. At the same time, momentous and emotionally supercharged incidents from the future may somehow reverberate "back" into the present.

The Amazing Alex Tanous

Astral travelers come in all shapes and sizes, their personalities ranging over a broad spectrum from introverted types to those who are gregarious and communicative. An example of the latter is Alex Tanous, a man who radiates friendliness and enthusiasm. Tanous is the favorite subject of many researchers because he is cooperative as well as talented. His out-of-body experiments at the American Society for Psychical Research promises to add considerably to our knowledge of OBEs and how they work.

Alex Tanous is one of a rare breed of astral projectors. Tanous is able to project at will. He says to himself, "Mind-go!" and then he finds himself in the present, past, or future at any time or place of his choosing.

Once, at a gathering of psychologists, Tanous went back to the Russian Revolution and described many of the historic scenes of 1917. He saw the revolutionaries, the soldiers, and the czar in the Winter Palace at Petrograd.

Tanous witnessed the unfolding of many events with which he was unfamiliar. He described where he was in broken English, as if he were a Russian translating from his native language. When Tanous visited Russia a few years later, the settings he had seen astrally looked exactly as they did in his projection.

Tanous' ability to make astral trips to the past has been put to such practical uses as locating missing persons and helping the police solve crimes. He does this by psychically going back to the place where the person or object was last seen and picking up the trail, following it as far as it leads him. In one instance he found a teacher in Florida who had been thought drowned when his boat was found on Lake Champlain in New York. In another he said that a hunter who had disappeared in a swampy area in Maine was alive but some distance away. The hunter was finally located in Iowa.

In other instances Tanous projects himself into the future, as he does when he makes predictions of world events. Two young German women visiting in Portland, Maine told Alex that they were looking for a house back home. Immediately he projected to Germany and saw a house by the water which he described to them. Later they wrote to thank him – they had found their "house by the water" and it was exactly as he had pictured it.

Since the Time-Space dimension as we know it does not exist on the astral plane, many of Tanous' projections give information from the past, present and future as if they were one. A nun and her sister once approached Tanous after a lecture and told him they were worried about their brother in Germany who had just been jailed on a charge of murdering his wife. Tanous suddenly found himself on the scene in Germany, witnessing all that had happened and seeing the outcome.

"Your brother is all right," he assured them. "He will not be convicted. He did not kill his wife and will be freed." As Tanous had predicted, their brother was absolved of the crime.

Tanous believes that he can travel the time dimension because his nonphysical self is a mass of energy, a ball of light.

This belief that he is a form of light energy when he leaves his body may be traced to a suggestion made by a priest in a school he once attended. It also gave him a clue to his astral trips to the past.

"If a man could throw himself into the light wave of something that happened a long time ago," said the priest, "he could be right there and witness what had happened."

It should be recalled that other projectors experienced themselves as masses of energy when out of their bodies, also that light from the second body frequently illuminates a dark room. Many projectors have found themselves in very bright light and brilliant color, especially when their astral environment was either of a symbolic nature or in a spiritual realm.

Tanous says also that he usually feels his "mass of energy" hovering over the place to which he has projected and that he doesn't receive his information directly – that is, through the senses – but that the spirit of which the energy is composed relays the information back to his physical body.

Human Time Machines

According to Gary S. Bekkum, Russian Physicist Michael Mensky, of the Lebedev Physical Institute, has revealed in a series of papers how human time machines are able to retrieve information from alternative worlds, including the future. Mensky, an associate of Russian time travel expert Igor Novikov, has proposed a model of the human time machine concept, based upon the "many worlds" interpretation of quantum theory.

The idea behind "many worlds," which now appears to be the simplest explanation of the theory behind 21st Century technology, says that the universe we observe is only one of an infinite number of invisible alternative worlds.

According to the quantum theory, as explained by leading expert David Deutsch, of Oxford, the worlds we cannot see weakly interfere with our universe. Quantum experiments confirm this interference, although the interpretation of the scientific observation of the effect is hotly debated by the scientific community.

Deutsch explains that among the alternative worlds are special worlds we call "the future." These worlds share a common past with our world, but branch off into different alternative events: As an example, in one of the alternative worlds the 9/11 attacks failed to take place.

In his landmark book, **The Fabric of Reality**, Deutsch describes how time machines might be used to connect the present moment with one of the future alternative worlds. According to Deutsch, information sent back in time from a future world could be used to change the future, since what we call the future is actually just a special case of an alternative parallel universe.

Mensky has proposed the idea of "post correction" to explain human time machines. In order to explain how human beings can become time travelers, Mensky developed an extended version of "many worlds" theory, where the human mind is able to access alternative worlds, including those we would call the future. Mensky has proposed that "consciousness is not produced by the brain, but is independent of it." In Mensky's theory, "the brain serves as an interface between consciousness and the body."

The human as living time machine would be the essence of the conscious experience: it proposes to answer the question of why we awaken to an experience of our senses, thoughts, memories, and existence. In the Many Worlds interpretation of Parallel Universes, other times, including future events, are viewed as special cases of different parallel universes.

For the human experience, the living time machine moves between different worlds by the action of the perception of those worlds. Typically, human consciousness demonstrates both a rate and a threshold of perception. Generally, it is accepted that we are typically

Time Travel – Fact Not Fiction

aware of events to about 1/10 of a second. If the human mind is a time machine, threaded by loops in time, we would expect those loops to correspond to the rate of our perception. The Many Worlds of Parallel Universes interpretation tells us that information moves backwards in time by connecting different parallel universes together.

The magical property of a time machine is an exotic sleight of hand. Information is processed in a different universe, which we call the future. All of the ordinary laws of physics apply. The work required to produce information, like tomorrow's newspaper, actually takes place in that other universe. News events occur, reporters research the day's events, editors assemble the daily news reports; all of the activity and energy required to produce the information occurs, but from the point of view of the present moment, everything required to assemble tomorrow's newspaper has taken place in a different world than the one in which we live.

The magic of the human time machine happens when our universe, the one we call the present moment, is connected to that other universe we call the future. All of the work required -- all of the day's events -- all of the energy and processes required -- took place in an alternative universe. The connection allows information about that other world to enter the world of the present moment. From our point of view, where our perception is focused on the present world, something truly magical takes place. A rabbit is pulled from an empty hat: the time machine transfers information from another universe to our own.

For the human as living time machine, self-perception emerges from the loops in time. The human mind passes from world to world as it loops through the Many Worlds of the Multiverse of Parallel Universes. This is a radical interpretation of the nature of consciousness: the human mind exists as a trans-universe process, literally beyond space and time. Although the loops in time would typically last less than a second, rapid enough to thwart conventional attempts to detect information transfer from the future world, under special circumstances one might imagine that loops might appear connecting alternative futures from tomorrow, next month, next year, and beyond.

Although Mensky's ideas appear to be based in metaphysics, the real-world application of human time travelers to access information about the future by the NSA suggests an information channel is being studied by America's premier information technology intelligence agency. Given the decades of interest in this topic by American and Russian, and now Chinese intelligence services, the on-going use of

Time Travel – Fact Not Fiction

human time machines to predict future threats seems certain. In 1994, the U.S. Defense Intelligence Agency contractor SAIC reported on a potential breakthrough in the physics of human time machines, following secret and covert analysis of research from the Former Soviet Union.

According to the SAIC report, the breakthrough involved the detection of a signal potentially related to the transmission and reception of information traveling through time. One source who came forward about the NSA program revealed the human time machines are managed under SIGINT, or Signals Intelligence, suggesting the program involves an unknown signal mechanism.nce, suggesting the program involves an unknown signal mechanism.

Camera To The Past

The suggestion that the astral body is made up of energy and is able to "tune in" to the past is similar to the beliefs of the late Father Alfredo Pellegrino Ernetti, an Italian monk who allegedly invented a device to tap into those past energies. Ernetti, who was born in 1926, was consumed by a passionate interest in what is called prepolyphony, archaic music composed from around 1400 BC to 1000 AD. Ernetti had become obsessed with the notion of finding out what the Roman opera Thyestes sounded like played on the musical instruments of its time.

The Italian monk approached a number of eminent scientists with an unusual proposition: Could they help him build a time machine to access these audio-visual musical performances now lost in time? Father Ernetti was convinced that such a machine could be built. Since time was energy, it must still exist somewhere. The machine would tap into these energy fields located beyond Time and Space.

He persuaded twelve scientists to help him develop and assemble what he would call a Chronovisor. The scientists contributed their expertise to the machine from the 1950s through the 1990s. A prototype of the Chronovisor is said to have been completed by the 1970s.

News was leaked about the Chronovisor in 1972 when a photo allegedly of Jesus dying on the cross was released to world newspapers. Father Ernetti remarked that he wondered if the Chronovisor was a blessing or a curse.

"The Chronovisor could be used to extract information from any part in history," explained Ernetti. "It was like an invisible spy that could be sent anywhere, anytime. It has the potential to reveal highly compromising information. If brought into full use, there would be no secrets left in the world."

Ernetti's concept for the Chronovisor had originated from a theory put forward by the Greek scientist Pythagoras in about 350 BC. Pythagoras suggested that the sounds of music broke down in such a way that they became atom-like particles that were stored in certain natural energy fields.

The late Baird T. Spalding, an American scientist who claimed that the Chronovisor had actually been developed, said that he had personally witnessed several successful experiments using the machine.

"Time travel is possible," said Spalding. "I observed in a place I will not mention, briefly, but definitively, events taking place in a long lost time."

Reportedly, the Catholic Church did not look favorably upon the idea of peering back into the mysteries of the past. On his superior's orders, Father Ernetti halted any further research into the Chronovisor and had the prototype disassembled and the parts permanently hidden away.

Do the past and future exist in a field of indestructible energy, able to be viewed and experienced under the proper conditions? If this notion is true, then we don't really need a machine like the Chronovisor to intercept these energies. The human mind should be able to do the same thing if properly trained and developed.

Use Your Natural Abilities To Locate Doorways Into Time

The Earth is constantly being bathed in a sea of energies. These natural forces not only rain down from outer space, but the planet itself produces magnetic energy that travels across the globe in the very same lines of force found in any toy magnet. These lines of force are extremely powerful. Under the right conditions, this energy can cause some very unusual things.

Located at various points on the planet there are areas of energy that create what could be called "faults" in the Time-Space continuum. These areas, also known as "windows" have a long history of strange happenings ranging from ghosts to repeated sightings of UFOs and weird monsters like Bigfoot. Could these areas be actual doorways into other dimensions or even time?

Dinosaur-like creatures, Bigfoot and other out-of-place animals that appear one day and disappear the next could be time travel events. Animals from the prehistoric past or the far future could be walking in and out of our reality through Time and Space doorways that occasionally open and close when the conditions are right. This could go a long way in explaining sightings of strange creatures by credible witnesses. These creatures may be able to exist in our time only for a short period until their energy is exhausted, sending them back to their original time.

These same doorways could also send someone from our time into the past or future. The problem is: How do we find these doorways? There are literally thousands of these "haunted" areas situated across the country. Chances are that there are several within a couple hours drive of your home. These are precise geographical locations, and anyone digging into the history and lore of such locations will find hundreds of accounts of ghosts, demons, monsters and UFOs pinpointed within a few square miles and covering a thousand years or more of time.

Paranormal activities and time slips in these areas seem to be controlled by complicated cyclic factors. Periodically, increased levels of activity in all of these places occur simultaneously, and we have a wave of strange disappearances, apparitions, monsters and UFO sightings. The window areas seem to be affected by strong electrical storms, sunspot activity, earthquakes, phases of the moon and other little understood natural events. Window areas tend to be places where peculiar magnetic faults exist. The planet is covered with magnetic faults. Interestingly enough, ancient mounds, temple sites and other sacred areas are usually grouped around magnetic fault locations.

A leading authority on mythology and mysticism, poet Robert Graves, stated: "There are some sacred places made so by the radiation created by magnetic ores. My village, for example, is a kind of natural amphitheater enclosed by mountains containing iron ore, which makes a magnetic field. Most holy places in the world -- holy not by some accident, like a hero dying or being born there -- are of this sort. Delphi was a heavily charged holy place."

In the Middle ages, the Vatican pointedly ordered that new churches should be constructed on the sites of old temples whenever possible. The tradition of sacred places runs deep and seems to be largely based upon the continuous observations of paranormal manifestations. The beings who allegedly approached human beings in miraculous events frequently ordered a church or temple to be built on the spot.

A magnetic survey of the United States was carried out by the government in the 1950s. Maps detailing magnetic variations in nearly every state can be obtained from the Office of Geological Survey in

Time Travel – Fact Not Fiction

Washington. Comparisons of the concentrations of paranormal manifestations with these maps show unique clusters around the magnetic aberrations.

There are now handheld models of electromagnetic monitors on the market that can be taken to these sites to check for peaks in electromagnetic activity. Periods of high electromagnetic energy should correspond with the openings of doorways. The doorways can appear anywhere and remain open for seconds to several minutes.

While the doorways are usually invisible, it has been reported that they can appear as areas of shimmering light, much like heat waves seen coming off of a hot road in the summer. Others have described the doorways as smoky or foggy patches, balls of light, or black holes hanging in the air. If you are close by you should experience a tingling sensation as if the air is supercharged with electricity. Oppressive and frightening is another description given by some who have experienced doorways.

If you are interested in trying to track down doorways in your area, you should first look for ancient Native American mounds or other structures. Contact your state's historical society or board of tourism for such areas. Practically any area will have several historical locations within an easy drive of your home. If you take the time to look up old records and newspaper accounts, you should find that these areas also have a high number of strange incidents over the years. Be sure to look for similar clusters of bizarre events in other areas in your state. They may not always be associated with ancient mounds and temples, they could be situated around a small town, in a local forest, an old churchyard or cemetery.

Once you have pinpointed several areas to investigate, you will have to spend some time getting to know the area. Study old and current local newspapers. Look for anything out of the ordinary. Try to establish a pattern of activity. This will help in establishing the best times when a doorway is likely to open. An instant camera is good to have along when you visit these sites. Simply take pictures of likely locations. Often strange foggy patches will appear on the developed film. These could show possible weak areas of magnetic force where a doorway could appear.

If you know someone who is psychic, invite them along for the hunt. Their natural abilities could be of great service in helping you pinpoint possible doorway areas. Above all, don't get discouraged. Many investigators have spent years in window areas with little to show for their efforts. Others have experienced unusual incidents within days of finding a possible locale.

Time Travel – Fact Not Fiction

Be aware that visiting such "haunted" areas can have unforeseen consequences for you afterwards. Don't be surprised if your home is visited by poltergeists or other ghostly phenomena. You could also experience weird phone calls, strange people coming to your door or stopping to talk to you on the street, and even increased UFO activity over your neighborhood.

Before tracking down any doorway area, you must consider whether this is what you really want to do. You could risk the chance of accidently falling through and getting lost in Time and Space. Some people have reemerged no worse from their experience. Others have disappeared forever. Are you willing to accept this grave risk?

Einstein postulated that if time and space were flat, then time travel would be possible. If the universe also contains an infinite number of parallel universes, then it could be possible to travel to these different realities by unleashing the amazing abilities of the human mind.

Chapter Nine
Personal Experiences With Time

If you are interested in time and the possibilities of traveling through it, then the chances are good that at some point in your life you will experience a strange event involving time. Weird slips in time, glimpses into the future, encountering the past, these unusual episodes occur on a daily basis throughout the world. Most tend to ignore anything out of the ordinary, while others are keenly aware that something strange has happened to them.

Jamie Stensrud writes about a strange incident that happened to him while he was attending St Mary's University at Halifax, Nova Scotia, Canada.

"It was daytime and I was home. The 'scene' just sort of popped into my head and lasted for maybe half a second (or less?). It was very vivid. I don't know how strange this will sound, but it was as if I was seeing from someone else's eyes, I was sitting on a chair or stool in a bedroom, in front of a large wooden bureau or dresser, with a large mirror attached to the back of it. There were items on the top of it, I got the impression they were various makeup or vanity items.

"I either had a brush in my hand, or there was one on the bureau. The texture of the walls was a dark brown or reddish-brown wood. I was getting ready to go out, and there was another person standing to the right, at the door, in retrospect I'd say maybe three or four meters away. He was dressed in a uniform, like a chauffeur, in black or dark blue, with buttons running up the front of the jacket, and he was wearing a hat of the same color, not a top hat or anything like that, but something more flat.

"I had the impression I was going out someplace, and that this person was an old friend, who was also in my employ. The reflection in the mirror was that of a female, I'd say in her 50's or early 60's, white, with shoulder length or just past shoulder length hair, either brown or some shade of red. She was of regular stature as far as I could tell, i.e., neither obese nor overweight. The mirror was large enough so that I could see her reflection from just above the top of her head to around her waist. The general feeling I got was that this woman was fairly well-off financially, and had a lot of time on her hands. I don't think there was anything outwardly indicating a time, but I 'knew' the chauffeur would be driving some kind of old-style (to us) car. If I had to place it in a time I'd say somewhere from 1920-1950, but I couldn't be sure. As I said, this impression was very quick, and even though I was looking at the woman's reflection in the mirror, I still 'knew' the other details, such as the man standing at the door, and his uniform. This was a one-time thing; I've never had anything like that happen since, but it was very vivid and something I'll remember for a long time."

Weird!

Andreas Klokkaris of Nicosia, Cyprus, remembers witnessing a strange slip in time when he was a child in 1987.

"When I was a kid, I was reading in the waiting room of a doctor's office, and I looked up and saw a man walking out of the door. I continued reading and after a couple of minutes I looked up again and saw exactly the same scene with the man walking out of the door as I saw it a few minutes before. Weird."

Tennis Anyone?

In 1996, Jeff V. and a friend, both from Cambridge, Massachusetts, decided to take some time off during the day to play a little tennis. They were in North Cambridge and didn't know where the nearest tennis courts were located.

"I pulled my car up to a police officer directing traffic around a small construction area on a side street. I asked him directions to the nearest courts. He gave clear instructions to courts only two blocks away. I followed his directions and pulled into a driveway. In front of us, we saw the courts quite clearly. We saw several people playing and looked at the courts quite intently as we were looking to find one free for us to play. We commented on the fact that everyone was wearing white. A lady in the right court wearing a white tennis dress seemed particularly attractive. I pulled the car to the parking area immediately on my right.

"You could imagine our surprise when we got out of the car and found everything we were looking at was gone! The entire area seemed to change in a moment. The courts were gone as was the field to the right. As well, the people that we had seen playing tennis

Time Travel – Fact Not Fiction

had just a mysteriously vanished. I found out later that there used to be tennis courts there, but they had been torn down 20 years before!"

Missing Time

Dawn Thomas, a housewife from Harlow in the county of Essex U.K., reports that in 1997 her son and a friend were taking a walk back from the rugby club which is about three miles away from their home. This usually took them half an hour to do but that night they were three hours late. Thomas and her husband were concerned considering that the two boys were walking through woods.

"We went across the road to see if they were back at the friend's house when they strolled around the corner, I shouted 'where the hell have you been?' but they looked at me strange saying 'what's wrong?' They looked at their watches to find three hours had gone by but they said it only seemed like half an hour. They said they had not detoured from their usual route that only took them half an hour. To this day I don't know where their missing time went."

Linking In Time

Stephen Voisey says that because of a popular book, he has been able to "link" forwards and backwards in time.

"I've 'linked' forwards, and backwards. What do I mean by linking? I first read about it in Richard Bachs book, *A Bridge Across Forever*, where he has very intense linking experiences, where he actually saw his future self and spoke to him. This happens about three times in the book, and I've always felt anything is possible, and tried the technique myself.

"I don't think it's hard, but it only works at specific times. Basically perhaps when you are feeling down, or thinking about your future self, I'd call this 'bookmarking,' where your future self will remember that time sometime in the future, and is thinking back about what they were like then. For instance, I was thinking about Richards idea, when I tried it. I saw myself on a beach, sitting crossed legged, meditating. What was my future self doing? Simply, I was sending a message back to myself here and now. What was the message, well, myself on the beach had a big smile on his face, and was not letting on, which is all I needed to know! That tells me everything, knowing myself as I do. Complicated...perhaps, but when you think about it, what's happening, is that our past and future selves are creating a temporary bridge. Of course there are specific bridges at certain points. It's not permanent, and it's not flexible. You can't just create a bridge unless your future self also does the same.

"It can also go the reverse way, your self NOW, creates a bridge to a past you, of course this has to happen at some point. I realize now that I have created several bridges to myself at key points in my life, and one crucially so. The farthest I went back, was several thousand years, and not alone either, I was with a good friend, I suppose you could call a soul mate, or soul family, etc.

"For some reason that night, we were both restless, and we started to spot the signs that spirit was trying to give us a message. We were trying to figure it out, when I began to see something. It was a massive temple, several kilometers away, the ground around it was bare with the occasional bush. I asked Steve what he could see, and he described the same. We realized we were both there, several thousand years ago."

Is Death A Jump In Time?

After what he thought was his death, Jake K. wonders if our consciousness, our Souls, are not jumping from Time and Space into other realities when death occurs.

"Years ago, my first brush with this phenomenon (that's what I call it) was hunting with my father in eastern Oregon. We had separated on a tracking venture, it had been hours since I had seen anyone in our party. Cresting a hill, I felt a sharp pain in my chest followed by the sound of a gunshot. I put my hand to my chest at the point of the pain. Looking down at my blood soaked hand I remember starting to fall as consciousness faded.

"The next thing I knew I was standing in the same spot at the crest of that hill looking at my hand remembering vividly events and pain that appeared not to have taken place. I dismissed this, after thinking about it I decided it had to have been my imagination, a daydream or something. I hypothesize that in most people death means a discontinuance of memory and a shift of dimensions to carry on the being or soul. A limitless branching universe that is always available for shifts to infinite parallels. I believe that these parallels are out there and that at the point of death in the universe I am in I shift to the new but retain memories from the last. The new universe changed only by the fact that circumstances leading to my death in the last had changed so that I did not meet an early end. But the points leading to the demise were not memory shifted but directly 'jerked' into the new consciousness."

Time Travel – Fact Not Fiction

Spacecraft Or Time Machines?

Many UFO investigators hold the theory that the UFO phenomena could represent time machines from our own future. Some UFO contactees report that the UFO occupants have said that their spacecraft actually travels the vast distances of the Universe by folding or pulling time around the craft. In essence, some UFOs are extraterrestrial craft and time machines.

In 1982 Lorraine Parry was walking in a suburban road in Wembley, North of London, when she felt a distinct change of surroundings. She describes seeing it as desert-like, though she perceived herself as standing in a lake. She could "feel" the wetness against her skin. While looking at the desert she saw something strange.

"I saw a craft going through the air. It was like an oblong shape. I think it must have been some kind of metal, it was silvery in color and it had some windows . . . I had the distinct feeling it was like a bus." She could see faces staring back at her, reminiscent of descriptions of aliens in several UFO reports. "They were all excited, and pointing, and I thought, 'they are pointing at me.'"

Lorraine's report is similar to the case of a British family traveling on an autobahn in Germany. They saw, passing on the other side, a long, silver, cylindrical vehicle with round portholes out of which four apparently equally startled faces were looking. They were not sure that the vehicle even had wheels and they heard no sound of engines. They watched the strange machine travel down the road behind them. Suddenly, the silvery vehicle seemed to become transparent and slowly faded away into nothingness.

A Car Lost in Time?

Ken Meaux, writing for the High Strangeness column in *Strange Magazine* number two, Spring 1988, relates another "car lost in time" story that he personally investigated. Meaux heard this strange tale from a friend of more than fifteen years, who was reluctant to repeat the curious story for fear of ridicule.

L.C. and a business associate, Charlie, (fictitious name) had just finished lunch in the small Southwest Louisiana town of Abbeville. Still discussing their work, they began their drive north along Highway 167 toward the Oil Center city of Lafayette about 15 miles away. The date was October 20, 1969, and the time was about 1:30 in the afternoon. It was a beautiful fall day, just the right conditions for cruising along with the car windows rolled down. The highway had been practically traffic-free until they spotted some distance ahead what appeared to be an old turtle-back-type auto traveling very slowly. As they closed the distance between their vehicle and this relic from the past, their discussion turned from their insurance work to the old car ahead of them. While the style of the auto suggested it to be decades old, it appeared to be in show room condition, which evoked words of admiration from both L.C. and Charlie.

Because the car was traveling so slowly, the two men decided to pass it, but before doing so, slowed to better appreciate the beauty and mint condition of the vehicle. As they did so, L.C. noticed a very large bright orange license plate with the year "1940" clearly printed on it. This was most unusual and probably illegal unless provisions had been made for the antique car to be used in ceremonial parades. However, neither man could remember if the plate listed an issuing state.

As they passed the car slowly to its left, L.C., who was in the passenger's seat, noticed the driver of the car was a young woman dressed in what appeared to be 1940 vintage clothes. This was 1969 and a young woman wearing a hat complete with a long colored feather and a fur coat was, to say the least, a bit unusual. A small child stood on the seat next to her, possibly a little girl. The gender of the child was hard to decide as it wore a heavy coat and cap that seemed more suited for the winter rather than October.

The windows of her car were rolled up, a fact which puzzled L.C. because, though the temperature was nippy, it was quite pleasant and a light sweater was sufficient to keep you comfortable. As they pulled up next to the car, their study turned to alarm as their attention was riveted to the animated expressions of fear and panic on the woman's face.

Driving alongside of her at a near crawl, they could see her frantically looking back and forth as if lost or in need of help. She appeared on the verge of tears. Being on the passenger's side, L.C. called out to her and asked if she needed help. To this she nodded "yes," all the while looking down (old cars sat a little higher than the low profiles of today's cars) with a very puzzled look at their vehicle. L.C. motioned to her to pull over and park on the side of the road. He had to repeat the request several times with hand signs and mouthing the words because her window was rolled up and it seemed she had difficulty hearing them.

They saw her begin to pull over so they continued to pass her so as to safely pull over also in front of her. As they came to a halt on the shoulder of the road, L.C. and Charlie turned to look at the old car behind them. However, to their astonishment, there was no sign of the car. Remember, this was on an open highway with no side roads nearby, no place to hide a car. It and its occupants had simply vanished.

L.C. and Charlie looked back at the empty highway. As they sat in the car, spellbound and bewildered, it was obvious to them that a search would prove futile. Meanwhile, the driver of a vehicle that had been behind the old car pulled over behind them. He ran to L.C. and Charlie and frantically demanded an explanation as to what had become of the car ahead of him.

He was driving North on Highway 167 when he saw, some distance away, a new car passing up a very old car at a slow pace, so slow that they appeared to be nearly stopped. He saw the new car pull onto the shoulder and the old car started to do the same. Momentarily, it obstructed the new car and then suddenly disappeared. He thought that an accident had occurred, but found nothing. This story, and others like it, makes one wonder if the woman and child from 1940 made it back to their own time, or instead, are still lost, forever driving the infinite highway somewhere between Time and Space.

Time Slip to the 1930s

This fascinating story comes from Stephen Wagner at paranormal.about.com. The author identifies herself as Joanne D.

My time slip experience took place in 1972 in New York. I was 18 and lived at my college dorm. It was July. My cousin had recently died and I was feeling melancholy. I decided to go for a three-block walk to the stores. I know for sure it was 3 p.m. when I left. As I crossed the street from my dorm and entered the first block, I noticed a deadening silence that got my attention. There was not a sound of life anywhere. That's when I noticed that the homes lining this residential street all were different: smaller and dated looking. (I'd guess around 1930s.) There were no cars anywhere and no driveways or garages, and everything seemed gray, without color. I noticed the trees were all bare, like in winter, yet this was summer. I spoke out loud saying, "Why is it so quiet?" And my voice seemed strange and tinny.

When I got to the main street with the stores, everything reverted back to normal, but upon returning home those three blocks took on the same strange qualities. Then I noticed that the entire side of the second block had a huge hill that wasn't there before, replacing all the houses.

As I exited the last block to go back to my dorm, everything was back to normal again -- Sound, movement, etc. I was gone about 90 minutes, but when I looked at the clock as I entered my room it said 3:12 p.m., which was only 12 minutes from when I left! I checked another clock and it also showed 3:12.

The next day, I took this same walk, and to my amazement it happened again. But on the return from the stores, the hill had now disappeared and was replaced with the older-looking homes (like on the first trip). After that day, the usual modern homes, sound, color, trees in full bloom were all back in place.

A Visit to Scotland, a Journey to the Past

This time-slip tale comes to us from John Carlson at his website: www.theparanomalist.com. The authors name is Linda Smith.

In 2004 I had grown absurdly fond of a PBS series, 'Monarch of the Glen', which was set in the highlands of Scotland. When I discovered that most of it was filmed in and around the village of Newtonmore and that Newtonmore was a regular stop on the main rail line to the North and Inverness, I simply had to go myself.

After a totally sleepless red-eye flight to London and another one to Glasgow, I finally got on the afternoon train for Inverness. Happily chatting with a group of friendly Scots, I nearly missed the stop. But I did swing off, the only passenger alighting. John, in spite of advancing age, I'm quite travel-oriented and love to travel solo where I can do and see entirely what I like.

I have traveled extensively in England and Scotland, Wales, and Ireland. But I have always encountered a rail station where I could ask directions if necessary. So, suitcase and carry-on in hand, I disembarked from the train at the Newtonmore station in Scotland. I swung onto the platform to meet absolutely nothing except a giant transformer in the center, surrounded by chain link fence with the polite British notice saying, 'Do not touch equipment. Danger of Death.' I sidled carefully around that and found myself looking out on open countryside. With the exception of a two-story Victorian style house that I took to the the stationmaster's — rather like a lighthouse keeper — there was simply nothing except open moorland. As I stood there in shock, a young man rode up on a bicycle. Of course, I asked, 'Sir, can you tell me which way the town is?' He stared silently at me for so long I had just concluded he was either a deaf mute or what the country people call 'a simple' and prepared to walk to the stationmaster's house. Just then he said vaguely, having looked around in every direction, '...it's not THAT way,' and pointed south in the exact direction I had come from. Rather than pointing this out, though, I asked, 'Could you tell me where the Glen Hotel is?' I had booked a room over the Internet, as it was seemingly the town's most popular. More confidently, he replied, 'No...no, there's no place like that around here' and promptly and swiftly rode away.

Frustrated, I dragged my luggage down the road to the 'station'. I was thrilled to see that the front door was open. As I approached the front yard, that door was suddenly and violently slammed shut from behind! I didn't know what to do — there was no other sign of civilization, but on the other hand I was so isolated I had no idea what I might encounter if I tried to pursue my information quest. I decided safety dictated that I should head up the only road there was, in the direction the man on the bike had gone. There were trees on the horizon, so there must be someone. And I couldn't see any other choice.

Accordingly, I set off. The train had arrived in typical British punctuality, at 6:32 p.m. Everything was unbelievably quiet, but I thought to myself, 'Lovely peaceful Scotland with its wonderfully kind people!' (all the more strange about the slamming door — not at all like the Scots I remember). Just then, at the first road to the right, a lorry came to the main road and turned right. I stopped and put on my best forlorn lost-tourist expression. To my shock, he looked right through me with no sign of recognition, let alone the expected query as to whether he could help me find directions!

I was astounded and started to hail him back, but just then I spied a young-looking woman about a block ahead of me. Thinking she would be more approachable, I hurried toward her. She was pushing what looked like an old-fashioned baby carriage ('pram' to the Brits) and, even with my wheeled suitcase, I hoped I could overtake her. I was horrified to see her look back, see me, and start hurrying away. I increased my pace the best I could, but the faster I walked the faster she did, and she got away from me, I suppose. I say 'I suppose' because that's the last thing I remember — after wondering why she acted scared of a little old lady dragging two suitcases! — until I found myself at the dead end of Station Road on the Main Street of Newtonmore.

I remember well thinking that the lights of the petrol station just ahead of me and the shops and buildings on down the road were the

Time Travel – Fact Not Fiction

most welcome sight I had ever laid eyes on! So I followed the hotel's website direction and directly found myself in the hotel lobby. I had to knock loudly on the kitchen door before locating someone to check me in. Inquiring about dinner in the hotel restaurant, I was told the dining room was closed for the night but that I could probably pick up something at the local grocery just down the street. I did just that, purchasing a packet of lovely farmhouse veg soup, pate, crackers, fruit, and a badly needed wee dram of local Scotch! I say all those details in the hope of convincing you that I do not customarily suffer from memory lapses...

Anyway, after a couple of days in the tiny village I decided to take an unexpected detour to Inverness for a couple of days; a local bus could take me from Main Street in front of the hotel straight into central Inverness. So I did not have to go back to that rail 'station'.

Now for the Twilight Zone part. I was in France (Rennes le Chateau area!) last year and had decided I didn't want to return to the US immediately), so I took the overnight sleeper to Scotland for a few days. After a lovely night in my tiny compartment, I woke early for our expected 8:30 Inverness arrival.

With a jolt I suddenly realized we would be going past Newtonmore; it's not only the main line to the North but the only one. I was thrilled to think of the Danger of Death transformer and the stationmaster's house again! We pulled to the station. It was in the middle of a bunch of buildings — residential-looking, for the most part. The station was a long, low building that obviously resembled what it was, an old Victorian rail station. Since no one boarded the train, we set off almost immediately while I sat frozen with shock. No transformer, no stationmaster's dwelling, and plenty of buildings where I would have certainly stopped for help had they been there!

I was weekending on the coast at Plockton, an atmospheric fishing village, and I wanted desperately to ask someone — anyone, about Newtonmore. Of course, they would have thought I was senile or worse, I assumed. Also, I rationalized that the station I saw was one further along and that we just didn't stop at Newtonmore since it might be only a Requet stop. But after I got home, I carefully counted the stops betwen Dalwhinnie and Inverness; there's less than half a dozen. So we had made the Newtonmore stop.

Then I went to Google Earth and looked on all those buildings along Station Road. I then checked the time of sunset in northern Scotland. I was stunned to find that it's around nine p.m. at the time of year, early May, that I was there. I had gotten off the train at 6:32. The trusty Internet tells me that village shops and pubs are a five- to ten-minute walk away. I found this from the Old Station's website, among others. That long, one story railway station had been closed awhile back and has been turned into a bed and breakfast, replacing a Victorian structure that burned down when a passing steam engine's spark sent it up in flames!

Somewhere, over three hours had vanished from my life. But that pales beside the contrast in the behavior of those four people as opposed to the normally hospitable, courteous behavior of the Scots! My next day in the village, in contrast, was absolutely filled with beautifully friendly and charming people. I simply can't help wondering: Could they have thought I was a ghost? I really think the truck driver, from his behavior, just didn't see me."

Time Travel – Fact Not Fiction

Weird slips in time, glimpses into the future, encountering the past, these unusual episodes occur on a daily basis throughout the world. Most tend to ignore anything out of the ordinary, while others are keenly aware that something strange has happened to them.

Chapter Ten
What Does Science Say About Time Travel?

In H.G. Wells' novel, The Time Machine, the hero jumped into a special chair, pushed a few buttons, pulled a lever and found himself shot several hundred thousand years into the future, where England has long disappeared and is now inhabited by strange creatures called the Morlocks and Eloi.

That may have made great fiction, but physicists have always scoffed at the idea of time travel, considering it to be the realm of cranks. However, rather remarkable advances in quantum gravity are reviving the idea that time travel is possible; it has now become fair game for theoretical physicists writing in the pages of Physical Review Magazine.

Not surprisingly, time travel has always been considered impossible. After all, Newton believed that time was like an arrow; once fired, it soared in a straight, undeviating line. One second on the earth was one second on Mars. Clocks scattered throughout the universe beat at the same rate.

Einstein gave us a much more radical picture. According to Einstein, time was more like a river, which meandered around stars and galaxies, speeding up and slowing down as it passed around massive bodies. One second on the earth was not one second on Mars. Clocks scattered throughout the universe kept time to their own set of special circumstances.

There are, however, certain quantities that do remain constant. These constants are related to four-dimensional quantities known as metric tensors. From this Einstein proved that Space and Time are two aspects of the same thing and that matter and energy are also two aspects of the same thing. From the second of these concepts we get the most famous equation in physics: $E=mc^2$. However, before Einstein died, he was faced with an interesting problem. Einstein's neighbor at Princeton, Kurt Goedel, perhaps the greatest mathematical logician of the past 500 years, found a new solution to Einstein's own equations

Time Travel – Fact Not Fiction

which allowed for time travel. The "river of time" notion now had whirlpools in which time could wrap itself into a circle. Goedel's solution was quite ingenious: it postulated a universe filled with a rotating fluid. Anyone walking along the direction of rotation would find themselves back at the starting point, but backwards in time. In his memoirs, Einstein wrote that he was disturbed that his equations contained solutions that allowed for time travel. He eventually concluded that the universe does not rotate, it expands (i.e., as in the Big Bang theory) and so Goedel's solution could be thrown out for "physical reasons."In 1963, Roy Kerr, a New Zealand mathematician, found a solution of Einstein's equations for a rotating black hole, which had bizarre properties. The black hole would not collapse to a point (as previously thought) but into a spinning ring (of neutrons). The ring would be circulating so rapidly that centrifugal force would keep the ring from collapsing under gravity. Anyone walking through the ring would not die, but could pass through the ring into an alternate universe.

Since then, hundreds of other "wormhole" solutions have been found to Einstein's equations. These wormholes connect not only two regions of space, but also two regions of time as well. In principle, they can be used as time machines. Maybe someone, somewhere is already doing this.

Recently, attempts to add the quantum theory to gravity has given some insight into the paradox problem. In the quantum theory, we can have multiple states of any object. For example, an electron can exist simultaneously in different orbits (a fact which is responsible for giving us the laws of chemistry). Similarly, Schrodinger's famous cat can exist simultaneously in two possible states: dead and alive. So by going back in time and altering the past, we merely create a parallel universe. So we are changing someone else's past by saving, say, John F. Kennedy from being assassinated in Dallas, but our Kennedy is still dead. In this way, the river of time forks into two separate rivers.

Time is a creation of the mind. However, it is not a figment of the imagination. Time is said to be limitless for no limit can be set to the possibility of things that exist in a progression. It is the measurement of change in things that exist. However, does this mean that we will be able to soon jump into a time machine, push a button and soar several hundred thousand years into the future? Not yet. There are still a number of difficult hurdles to overcome.

The main problem is one of energy. In the same way that a car needs gasoline, a time machine needs to have incredible amounts of energy. One either has to harness the power of a star, or to find

Time Travel – Fact Not Fiction

something called "exotic matter" (which falls up, rather than down) or find a source of negative energy. (Physicists once thought that negative energy was impossible. But tiny amounts of negative energy have been experimentally verified for something called the Casimir effect, i.e., the energy created by two parallel plates). All of these are exceedingly difficult to obtain in large quantities, at least for several more centuries.

Then there is the problem of stability. The Kerr black hole, for example, may be unstable if one falls through it. Similarly, quantum effects may build up and destroy the wormhole before you enter it. Unfortunately, our mathematics are not powerful enough to answer the question of stability because you need a Unified Field Theory which combines both quantum forces and gravity. Right now, superstring theory is the leading candidate for such a theory.

Interestingly enough, Stephen Hawking once opposed the idea of time travel. He even claimed he had "empirical" evidence against it. If time travel existed, he said, then we would have been visited by tourists from the future. Since we see no tourists from the future, ergo: time travel is not possible. Because of the enormous amount of work done by theoretical physicists within the last five years or so, Hawking has since changed his mind, and now believes that time travel is possible (although not necessarily practical).

The general theory of time travel is that most events are regulated by what is called the Circular Theory of Time. In this theory one is required to picture the Space-Time continuum as a "laser disk," a circular plane with a starting point at the center. The creation of the universe is dubbed Event One, and it is this that the center of the disc represents. As time passes everything moves out in a spiral fashion until the boundary is reached. At the boundary it is theorized that time runs backwards (the Universal Entropy State) and all event waves now head toward Event One.

One important factor of this theory is the idea that there is something that represents everyone and everything in the universe . Every person has an event wave that signifies his/her life. No event wave, no existence. Without consciousness there is no universe. Add together all the PEWs for one period in time and an origin wave is formed, the sum of all PEWs. The circular theory of time allows a PEW to be separate from an origin wave and depositing it in another point in the space-time dimension.

A person's present time is defined by their origin wave. This origin wave is composed of an infinite number of personal event waves (PEWs). For every individual there is a PEW, which signifies the existence of that person in any dimension. Absolute present cannot be

Time Travel – Fact Not Fiction

defined as it never exists. However, what can be defined is a relative, flexible present. This is the notion of the existence of a defined time band in which any period can be classed as one's present time zone. Time, like space, although a dimension in itself, has dimensions of its own. These extra time dimensions represent other realities. Realities which alter because of time travel. The circular theory states that by moving back in time and changing events, a new future is mapped out from the point of interference. This alternative time dimension could diverge little from established history, or it could be wildly different from the normal time.

By altering a past event, the events that did happen still occur, but in a different dimension of time. Thinking back to the circular theory, it is like having two or more laser disks. These alternative realities, parallel time dimensions, are created when an alternative reality wave (ARW) diverges from the normal reality stream (NRS).

Because of this effect any change made to history will affect the present and future of all individuals concerned. Once history has been interfered with and the meddler returns to his present, he will return to a parallel present which has diverged from the NRS. This is unavoidable, as there is no way right now to work against this temporal "gravity."

However, Quantum Physics has shown that you do not need a time traveler to cause branching time lines in reality. The simple process of observation is enough to create an infinite number of universes from the very moment of conscious observation.

In effect this shows that reality has a built-in mechanism to prevent a paradox from ever happening. This could never happen if time travel wasn't already occurring continuously as a result of natural whirlpools in the time steam that rub against each other and occasionally force open doorways in Time and Space.

Existence of Parallel Universes Boosts Time Travel Hopes

Parallel universes really do exist, according to a mathematical discovery by Oxford scientists that sweeps away one of the key objections to the mind boggling and controversial idea.

The work has wider implications since the idea of parallel universes sidesteps one of the key problems with time travel. Every since it was given serious lab credibility in 1949 by the great logician Kurt Godel, many eminent physicists have argued against time travel because it undermines ideas of cause and effect to create paradoxes: a

Time Travel – Fact Not Fiction

time traveler could go back to kill his grandfather so that he is never born in the first place. But the existence of parallel worlds offers a way around these troublesome paradoxes, according to David Deutsch of Oxford University, a highly respected proponent of quantum theory, the deeply mathematical, successful and baffling theory of the atomic world.

He argues that time travel shifts between different branches of reality, basing his claim on parallel universes, the so-called "many-worlds" formulation of quantum theory. The new work bolsters his claim that quantum theory does not forbid time travel.

"It does sidestep it. You go into another universe," he said yesterday, though he admits that there is still a way to go to find schemes to manipulate space and time in a way that makes time hops possible.

"Many science fiction authors suggested time travel paradoxes would be solved by parallel universes but in my work, that conclusion is deduced from quantum theory itself," Dr Deutsch said, referring to his work on many worlds.

The mathematical idea of parallel worlds was first glimpsed by the great quantum pioneer, Erwin Schrodinger, but actually published in 1957 by Hugh Everett III, when wrestling with the problem of what actually happens when an observation is made of something of interest - such as an electron or an atom – with the intention of measuring its position or its speed.

In the traditional brand of quantum mechanics, a mathematical object called a wave function, which contains all possible outcomes of a measurement experiment, "collapses" to give a single real outcome. Everett came up with a more audacious interpretation: the universe is constantly and infinitely splitting, so that no collapse takes place. Every possible outcome of an experimental measurement occurs, each one in a parallel universe.

If one accepts Everett's interpretation, our universe is embedded in an infinitely larger and more complex structure called the multiverse, which as a good approximation can be regarded as an ever-multiplying mass of parallel universes.

Every time there is an event at the quantum level - a radioactive atom decaying, for example, or a particle of light impinging on your retina – the universe is supposed to "split" into different universes.

A motorist who has a near miss, for instance, might feel relieved at his lucky escape. But in a parallel universe, another version of the same driver will have been killed. Yet another universe will see the motorist recover after treatment in hospital. The number of alternative scenarios is endless. In this way, the "many worlds" interpretation of quantum mechanics allows a time traveler to alter the past without producing problems such as the notorious grandfather paradox. But the "many worlds" idea has been attacked, with one theoretician joking that it is "cheap on assumptions but expensive on universes" and others that it is repugnant to common sense." Now new research confirms Prof Deutsch's ideas and suggests that Dr Everett, who was a PhD student at Princeton University when he came up with the theory, was on the right track.

Commenting in *New Scientist* magazine, Prof Andy Albrecht, a physicist at the University of California, Davis, said of the link between probability and many worlds:

"This work will go down as one of the most important developments in the history of science."

Quantum mechanics describes the strange things that happen in the subatomic world – such as the way photons and electrons behave both as particles and waves. By one interpretation, nothing at the subatomic scale can really be said to exist until it is observed. Until then, particles occupy nebulous superposition states, in which they can have simultaneous "up" and ""down" spins, or appear to be in different places at the same time.

According to quantum mechanics, unobserved particles are described by "wave functions" representing a set of multiple "probable" states. When an observer makes a measurement, the particle then settles down into one of these multiple options.

But the many worlds idea offers an alternative view. Dr Deutsch showed mathematically that the bush-like branching structure created by the universe splitting into parallel versions of itself can explain the probabilistic nature of quantum outcomes. This work was attacked but it has now had rigorous confirmation by David Wallace and Simon Saunders, also at Oxford.

Dr Saunders, who presented the work with Wallace at the Many Worlds at 50 conference at the Perimeter Institute for Theoretical Physics in Waterloo, Canada, told New Scientist:

"We've cleared up the obscurities and come up with a pretty clear verdict that Everett works. It's a dramatic turnaround and it means that people now have to discuss Everett seriously." Dr Deutsch added that the work addresses a three-century-old problem with the idea of probability itself, described by one philosopher, Prof David Papineau, as a scandal.

"We didn't really know what probability means," said Dr Deutsch.

There's a convention that it's rational to treat it for most purposes as if we knew it was going to happen even though we actually know it need not. But this does not capture the reality, not least the 0.1 per cent chance something will not happen.

"So," said Dr Deutsch, "the problems of probability, which were until recently considered the principal objection to the otherwise extremely elegant theory of Everett (which removes every element of mysticism and double-talk that have crept into quantum theory over the decades) have now turned into its principal selling point."

Visits From Time Travelers

The theoretical evidence for time travel is considerable. There is, however, one question that those skeptical of time travel continuously ask: "If time travel is possible, where are the time travelers?" There are a number of possibilities. The most obvious and pessimistic of these is that life on Earth may not survive long enough for the technology to evolve. Nuclear wars, being hit by comets and asteroids, disease, etc. These all could stop mankind from progressing far enough to develop time travel.

Yet the absence of time travelers need not suggest anything nearly so sinister. It is possible that they have been here, and are here right now, but have been discreet about their presence. A further possibility is simply that none has arrived in this particular universe. Even stranger is the theory that UFOs and the entities that pilot them could, in fact, be time travelers from the future.

The idea that UFOs, rather then representing extraterrestrial beings, could be time machines is not a new consideration. What better way could a future race hide their origins than by insinuating that they are aliens from other planets to anyone who has come in contact with them.

Creatures seen by UFO witnesses are almost always described as basically humanoid. Considering the extremely wide range of life just on planet Earth, it is highly unlikely that intelligent creatures that evolved on planets light years from Earth would ever develop physically identical to humans. Plus, the so-called aliens seem to know an awful lot about us and our history. The recent descriptions of certain UFO entities with their grey skin, small, frail bodies and large

Time Travel – Fact Not Fiction

heads certainly seem like the popular notion of what man may look like in the far future.

The existence of a time machine would radically change our lives and society like no other event in recorded history. No longer would there have to be a "road not taken," we could simply travel back in time and make some other choice. If that choice didn't work out, we could go back into the past and try again. In a time-traveling society, our actions would no longer be irreversible.

A time machine would open every moment in history to scientific scrutiny, conferring on its users a kind of temporal omniscience. The time machine would provide more than mere knowledge of past events, it would actually transport its occupants bodily into an earlier time, where we could experience past historical events directly, enjoying a potential omnipresence beyond the reach of those still caught in time's usual one-way flow.

A time machine, however, is apparently not really necessary to journey across time. Time appears to be adaptable enough to allow people to deliberately or accidently leave their current time line and interact with others. More-than-likely this is occurring continuously across the multi-universes. Self-awareness and the power of the mind are all that is really needed to break down the barriers of Time and Space. Spiritual masters have been telling us for centuries that time is simply an illusion created by the brains need for patterns and order. Existence is a continuous state of Now.

The past, present and future all exist at the same time, and all three can be changed with the conscious efforts of individuals. Our minds, which are separate from physical reality, exist in a perpetual state of timelessness. Because of this, the lives you live in the past, the life you live now, and your future lives, are all occurring right now at the very moment you are reading these words. You can visit these times anytime you want. You just have to learn to forget what the physical body has taught us for generations - that time is unchangeably flowing into the future.

We are not prisoners of Time and Space. Rather, we are prisoners of our physical bodies and the learned behaviors of existing in the material world. The Universe and all of its mysteries await those who are not afraid to throw off the shackles of unawareness and begin the eternal quest of exploration and learning, advancing the evolution of our Souls and bringing us together once again with Creation.

Chapter Eleven
UFOs and Time Distortion

For most people, spotting a UFO would be considered extremely unusual, but for two Ohio women, seeing a UFO was the least surprising part of their experience.

In June 2001, two sisters, Angie Whitmeyer and Deborah Simmons, were returning from a day of shopping in Dayton, Ohio, when a strange light in the sky caught their attention.

"We were heading home to Kingman, Ohio, on State Road 73," Deborah recalled. "It was a beautiful evening around 8:30 p.m., the air was warm and the sky crystal clear. Angie was driving and I was watching the scenery go by when I noticed a bright light in the western sky."

Deborah watched in amazement as the light grew in intensity and flew towards the car at an incredible speed.

"Deborah asked me what that weird light was," said Angie. "But we were close to Caesar Creek Lake and the road was pretty dark so I wasn't paying a lot of attention to it. But then it flew right in front of us so I couldn't miss it."

The bright light soared past the car and hovered over the nearby treetops, casting an eerie glow over the entire area. Whitmeyer pulled the car over onto the side of the road so they could get a better look at the unusual object.

Deborah was shocked by how large and close the UFO was to them: "The light was so bright and white that you couldn't see any shape behind it. But we could tell it was pretty big, at least as big as a house. The funny thing was that I couldn't hear any sort of engine like you would normally hear with an airplane or helicopter. It was completely silent."

Suddenly, another, identical bright light swooped down from the sky and hovered a short distance away. The two sisters decided the situation was becoming too strange and tried to drive away.

Time Travel – Fact Not Fiction

"That's when I discovered that the car had stopped and I couldn't restart it," Angie said. "Nothing worked, the lights, the radio, it was completely dead."

The two women also noticed an odd silence had descended over the area, accompanied by a strange feeling of isolation. Angie remembered that it seemed as if they were the only people in the world.

"I don't remember seeing another car come by during the entire time we were there, which is really weird because at that time of an evening there's always traffic on that road. And it was just dead silent outside, no birds, nothing. It was as if we were in another world."

Uncertain what to do next, Angie and her sister continued to watch the strange pair of lights, when, unexpectedly, both objects shot straight up and disappeared into the night sky. The area was plunged into darkness, and oddly enough, the normal sounds of the night came back almost as if switched on.

"As soon as the lights flew away," Deborah said, "the car started running again all by itself. The lights and radio were on just as they were before everything happened."

According to their watches, the strange encounter had lasted more than 20 minutes. However, when they arrived home, Deborah's husband seemed unconcerned about what they thought was a late arrival. That's when they discovered that instead of being after 9:00 p.m., as their wristwatches indicated, it was only 8:35 p.m.

"It was as if the entire time we spent looking at those lights had never happened," Angie said. "But it did happen, our watches both showed we had been stuck out there for over 20 minutes, but somehow we gained that time back with a few minutes to spare. Normally we should have been home at around ten to nine, but somehow, despite what had happened, we got there early."

Distortions in Time and Space

One of the strangest aspects of some UFO encounters is the apparent distortion of time when a UFO is nearby. Researchers and writers have tried for years to understand and to interpret what happens before, during, and after a close contact with a UFO. But, many reports of time anomalies have been kept off some UFO databases because such events fall outside of the preconceived notions of what a UFO sighting should entail. Like the two Ohio sisters, others who have experienced a close contact with a UFO have reported apparent time distortions like

154

the failure of car engines, a strange feeling of isolation (to the point where it is observed that no other vehicles or people are seen during the sighting), unusual silence, spatial changes, altered states of consciousness, and distortions in the flow of time.

Generally, these anomalies disappear along with the UFO. Occasionally, however, the witnesses will suffer from unexpected relapses weeks, even years, after the initial experience.

These anomalous events have created more headaches than answers for researchers who have attempted to find scientific validation for unusual UFO encounters. On the surface, some of the reported anomalies seem to be explainable using modern science. However, upon closer analysis, strange things tend to become even stranger.

Failure of Car Engines

The disruption of car motors, machinery, and electronic devices during a UFO event has been commonly reported. Thousands of these inexplicable stories have been duly recorded over the years and many volumes have been written in an attempt to understand the underlying principles involved.

Mark Rodeghier of the Center for UFO Studies analyzed 441 cases in which "the car, truck, or other motor vehicle in which a witness was either riding or in near proximity to, was seemingly affected by the presence of a UFO. Headlights, radios and even flashlights were also affected."

Of the vehicle failure cases summarized by Rodeghier, ten percent noted an unusual phenomenon called "spontaneous engine restarts" at the end of a sighting. In reality, this figure is probably much higher considering the amount of underreported and under documented cases worldwide.

In these cases the car's engine would mysteriously restart without the driver turning the key. One witness said: "As soon as the UFO flew away, the car, radio, headlights, switched back on by themselves. One second everything was completely dead, and the next, everything was running smoothly as if nothing had ever happened."

The witness said he was left with the feeling that his car had been stopped between the ticks of a clock: "Like time had completely vanished."

Another notable feature of many cases is the sudden unusual silence and an overwhelming feeling of isolation in the proximity of a UFO. Many people have noted that normal sounds—birds, insects, traffic—suddenly stop just before and during a close UFO sighting. A man from Wisconsin reported that he had observed a UFO hovering over the treetops directly over his head once while deer hunting. He stated that the day had been windy and the trees were swaying and creaking pretty loudly in the breeze. What made him look up was the fact that all of a sudden the forest went "completely dead."

He noted that the trees had stopped moving as if "frozen in place." That is when he noticed a strange, dark, triangle-shaped object floating over the trees.

"It was a little bigger than a pickup truck and was solid black. I didn't see any lights or hear any kind of sound from it."

The hunter reported feeling like he was "looking up through a tunnel with me at the bottom and the UFO at the top. I knew that I was completely alone and that no one could help me."

As soon as the UFO passed overhead the forest returned to normal.

The experience of such unusual sensations around a UFO has been dubbed "the Oz Effect" by UFO researcher and author Jenny Randles, and may indicate that there could be a field of influence that is being emitted around a UFO. Anyone close enough to a UFO would find himself completely contained within this field. The odd effects noticed by eyewitnesses could give us some kind of indication of the true nature of these energy fields. Unfortunately, anecdotal accounts of UFO experiences have rarely been followed up with rigorous studies of their content.

UFOs and Time

Scientists brave (or foolhardy) enough to try and conduct proper research on the nature of UFOs have been unable to find satisfactory answers as to why UFOs seem to cause time distortions. Past interpretations of Einstein's physics leave little room for localized time anomalies, unless influenced by a gravitationally massive object such as a black hole.

However, the new kids on the physics block, quantum and string theories, may show that time and space are easier to influence than was previously thought. Some physicists believe that it is possible to engineer space-time itself and to surround a spaceship with a local space-time in such a way that locally, the light barrier remains intact, while from the outside the ship is moving at faster-than-light velocity. UFOs that seem to rapidly accelerate, change direction, or even disappear are actually operating conservatively from the viewpoint of their own internal time rates.

If someone or something came close enough to a ship that was creating its own space-time, normal time and space, as they know it, would cease to exist for them, and they would come under the influence of the artificial space-time.

This could explain some of the stranger aspects of UFO encounters, such as environmental sounds disappearing, isolation, the freezing of motors and electronic devices, and the feeling of time slowing down, stretching out, and losing all meaning. The UFO is literally creating an alteration in the local state of space-time, thus generating a major distortion effect that is experienced by the witness. Within this time anomaly the perceived forward motion of time could even disappear, allowing for the past, present, and future to intrude upon one another.

A Glimpse of the Past

In 1981, Linda Taylor and her mother were traveling by car to Chorlton, a district of Manchester, England. The normally busy road became strangely empty and the two women noticed a huge light in the sky that seemed to pace their car.

Linda told investigators that her car "jerked about" and slowed down despite her attempts to accelerate. Suddenly, an "old-fashioned" car appeared in the road ahead and drove straight towards the two women. At the same time the light in the sky turned into a metal disc that hovered over the main road.

As the UFO moved away from Taylor and her mother, the old car vanished instantly. When the women returned home they found that two hours were missing from their trip. As with some others who have had close UFO encounters, Linda later had several odd psychic experiences and further time lapses.

Time distortions may not always occur with a visible UFO nearby. In 1980, Peter Rojcewicz, now a professor of humanities and folklore at New York's Juilliard School, was in the University of Pennsylvania library reading a UFO book suggested by another professor.

As he read, Rojcewicz noticed that someone was standing in front of him. Looking up, Rojcewicz saw a very gaunt, pale man, about six feet tall and weighing around 140 pounds. The strange man wore a black suit, black shoes, a black string tie, and a bright white shirt. His suit was loose and it looked as though he had slept in it for days.

Time Travel – Fact Not Fiction

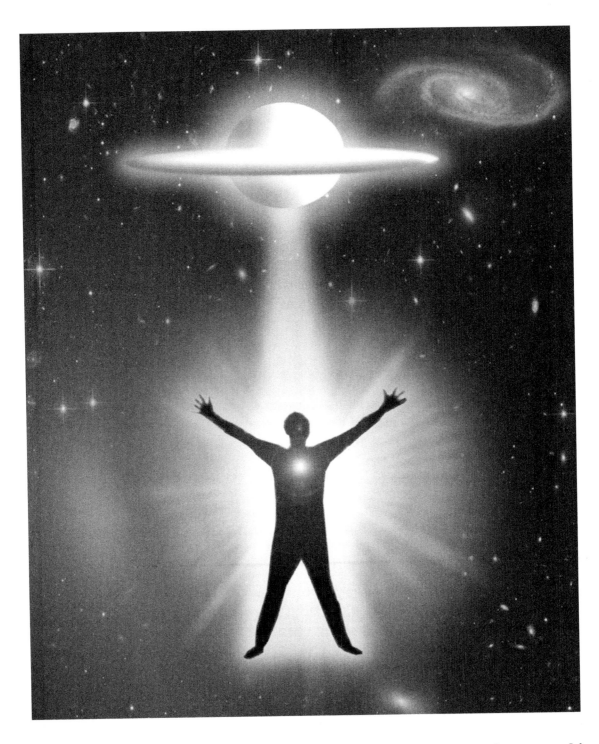

It could be that UFOs are using a propulsion system that surrounds a spaceship with a local space-time in such a way that locally, the light barrier remains intact, while from the outside the ship is moving at faster-than-light velocity. In other words, UFOs are time machines.

Time Travel – Fact Not Fiction

"He sat down like he had dropped from the ceiling—all in one movement—and folded his hands on top of a stack of books in front of him," Rojcewicz said. The man asked Rojcewicz what he was doing. Rojcewicz said he was reading about flying saucers.

"Have you seen a flying saucer?" the man asked. Rojcewicz said he hadn't.

"Do you believe in the reality of flying saucers?" Rojcewicz said he didn't know much about them and wasn't sure he was very interested in the phenomena.

The man screamed: "Flying saucers are the most important fact of the century and you are not interested?"

The man then stood up, again, all in a single awkward movement, put his hand on Rojcewicz's shoulder, and said: "Go well on your purpose." With that, he left.

Rojcewicz was suddenly overwhelmed by fear: "I had a sense that this man was out of the ordinary and that idea frightened me. I got up and walked around the stacks toward where the reference librarians usually are. The librarians weren't there. There were no guards there—there was nobody else in the library...I was utterly alone and terrified."

The professor went back to the table where he had been reading "to get myself together. It took me about an hour. Then I got up and everything was back to normal; the people were all there."

It would seem that Rojcewicz could have been placed into a separate time-space field in order for his contact to occur. The entire episode may have occurred in the blink of an eye in normal time-space. But for Rojcewicz, an entire hour passed.

One gentleman, who reported his alleged UFO abduction on an Internet forum, said that when he was being returned from an abduction to the motel room where he was staying, he "noticed that there was a person in the parking lot below us (myself and several 'Grays,' were 'floating' in mid-air so I had a bird's eye view of the surroundings,) [who] seemed to be frozen in mid-step. Everything was dead quiet and nothing was moving. It was as if time had stopped or frozen for the few moments it took for them to transport me from a UFO back to my room that was located on the second floor of the motel."

These interesting cases show that there is still a lot we have to learn from UFO reports. Investigators need to be willing to look beyond the traditional "by-the-book" questions and allow the witnesses to relate their entire experience—no matter how unusual it may be.

Time Travel – Fact Not Fiction

Many researchers and databases fail to mention some of the stranger aspects of UFO encounters because they don't fit a particular belief system or bias. We can learn much more if researchers put aside their own personal feelings and allow the full information to come forward.

The Roswell Time Machine

After his book, **The Day After Roswell**, had been published, Col. Phillip Corso alluded several times to the possibility that UFOs used an exotic propulsion system that essentially made them time machines. In 2004, Corso's son, Phil Corso Jr. spoke with the co-author of **The Day After Roswell**, William Birnes, at Stephen Bassett's X-Conference. What was stated by both of them was that the UFO that crashed near Roswell in 1947 was not an extraterrestrial spaceship, but was instead a time machine.

Of particular interest was information about the so-called Extraterrestrial Biological Entities – which contained two brains. One was organic and thought to control the beings, and one was "laced with crystal electronics" that is still not understood to this day, which was thought to connect the beings with the craft – through time.

It is purported that these beings are essentially Artificial Intelligences from our own future – and that their "crash" caused a bifurcation of our time-lines and altered our history. The most mind-boggling aspect of this story and the theory that the Air Force etc are operating under, is that as a result of this time-line split and the subsequent advancement in technology from reverse-engineering, that we (or the military) are now on a time-line of technological evolution that will eventually create the very same craft and beings that actually crashed in Roswell in 1947

Currently, any theories and conclusions about UFOs and time travel are really little more than speculation. Nevertheless, scientists who are not afraid to look beyond the norm are currently developing new concepts in physics and the true nature of reality.

Time Travel – Fact Not Fiction

Write for our FREE catalog of fascinating books, mind-bending DVDs, out of this world audio CDs, and other items of interest. Send your name and mailing address to:

Global Communications

P.O. Box 753

New Brunswick, NJ   08903

Email: mrufo8@hotmail.com

www.conspiracyjournal.com

Printed in Great Britain
by Amazon